A CUP OF WATER

A CUP OF WATER

A CUP OF WATER

The Story of Christian Aid

by

JANET LACEY

HODDER AND STOUGHTON

Printed in Great Britain for Hodder and Stoughton Limited, St. Paul's House, Warwick Lane, London, E.C.4. by Richard Clay (The Chaucer Press), Ltd., Bungay, Suffolk

To Marjorie and Scott Wilkie
with love and many thanks
for providing a home background

FOREWORD

By Professor Sir Robert Birley

I FIRST met Janet Lacey in Berlin in the spring of 1947. I had just been appointed Educational Adviser in the British Zone of Germany. I thought it would be a good plan to hold in Berlin a meeting of those in the British Zone who were engaged in work for German youth. Janet Lacey attended the meeting. In a short time I learnt a good deal about her—but not everything.

To begin with, I was in some doubt whether she had any right to be there at all. She was, I thought, supposed to be dealing with the British forces. But somehow she had used this position to do an extraordinary amount for German young people. Then, it was not at all easy to find out what her official position was. All this I learnt later on was quite typical. The difficulty has been that she has usually held so many different posts at once that it was often not at all easy to tell which one she was filling at any one moment. Not that it mattered much. She did what she was convinced she ought to be doing and the official position was moulded accordingly. I might add that she did not seem to be taking me very seriously. In fact, it appeared to me that throughout my opening address she was talking to her neighbour. But she has never taken Chairmen of Conferences very seriously.

Later I became aware of her remarkable energy. With this is combined an equally remarkable administrative efficiency. Now, one meets energetic people and unorthodox people and efficient people, but it is rare to meet them making up one person. Add to that the power to speak forcefully and clearly. (Looking back on it, it seems almost inevitable that she was the first woman to preach in St. Paul's and Liverpool Cathedral and St. George's Cathedral in Jerusalem.) Does all this sound rather alarming? If so, something important has been omitted. For, to use a hackneyed phrase, she is exceedingly good company.

It is good that she has written a book about her experiences. For she has played a vital part in some of the most important movements and problems of the last twenty-five years, the ecumenical movement, the problem of refugees, the problems of world poverty and hunger, the problem of race relations. She has inspired thousands of people to work to solve them and she has organised their efforts. In her odd spare moments she has helped all kinds of other activities. I myself shall never forget how she helped to launch Voluntary Service Overseas: it would never have got to sea without her. Bureaucracy has collapsed at her approach; no one ever broke more rules. In a very small way, I shall not forget how when I was in Africa and came across what seemed to me to be a desperate need which could not be met, I automatically wrote to her. Almost more remarkable than her response through Christian Aid was the speed with which it came.

This book will make clear what a recital of her activities might fail to disclose—that she is no 'battle-axe'. She is kind and amusing and interested in all kinds of things outside her work. She has done more than most people in her generation to make Christianity a living and relevant issue. Her very many friends will be delighted through this book to share her with others.

ROBERT BIRLEY

ACKNOWLEDGEMENTS

The extract from Sydney Carter's poem 'The Miracle' is quoted from *Nothing Fixed or Final*, © Sydney Carter 1969, published by Galliard Ltd.

The extract from Tom Paxton's 'Can't Help But Wonder Where I'm Bound' is reproduced by permission of Harmony Music Ltd.

The extracts from W. H. Auden's 'Refugee Blues' are quoted from the *Collected Shorter Poems*, 1927–1957, by W. H. Auden, published by Faber & Faber Ltd.

CONTENTS

INTRODUCTION

THE suggestion by colleagues that I should write a book about the first twenty years of Christian Aid proved to be much more difficult a task than I had anticipated. There was a mountain of material and therefore selection was difficult and while it would have been easy to chronicle a list of projects and names of workers, this would have been unsatisfactory. The real problem was how to convey to well-fed and well-housed men and women of goodwill the human agony of being permanently hungry. I have not experienced that, although I have seen the results of it in many parts of the world. How to explain without using sentimental clichés, the terrible personal problems of large numbers of people constantly dependent on 'Charity', or the bewilderment of stateless and lonely people—which persists until death—when they are forced to live in a foreign community with a different culture and are permanently misunderstood?

Clearly this was an impossible task but it is my hope that the reader will catch a hint of what it means to be a refugee, or to have to feed a family on two shillings and sixpence a day. If some readers get a notion of what can be done by governments, churches and sympathetic men and women to narrow the gap between the rich and poor nations through sacrifice and political action, then I shall rest content.

Inevitably, I have been obliged to quote extensively from various Christian Aid pamphlets and reports produced by me and others during the years. Most particularly I wish to record my thanks to Mr. V. K. Littlewood for his detailed work on the report of the 'Freedom from Hunger Campaign'. He and Mr. B. J. Dudbridge, the Deputy Director, were and still are of outstanding value to the whole enterprise.

I am most grateful to staff members of Christian Aid for material and comments and more particularly to the Rev. A. Alan Brash, who succeeded me as Director of Christian Aid in 1968. He was not only helpful but enthusiastic that I should make an effort to write the story of this modern Christian voluntary organisation.

Without the encouragement of my old friend and colleague, the Rev. Kenneth Slack, I would never have persevered to the end. He spent a long time reading the first draft and advised me how best to put it into shape. I am more than grateful.

Dr. Elfan Rees of the World Council of Churches wrote a booklet some years ago called *Century of the Homeless Man*. He, and others in the same context, have often quoted A. E. Houseman and I make no apologies in doing the same.

> *'And how am I to face the odds*
> *Of man's bedevilment and God's?*
>
> *I, a stranger and afraid*
> *In a world I never made.'*

I

A PERSONAL PROLOGUE

A PERSONAL PROLOGUE

I RETIRED from Christian Aid in the Spring of 1968 and in the summer finished my responsibilities with the World Council of Churches. I then had the leisure to look back in time, and to assess the immediate extraordinary experience I had had during the earlier months of the year. It also gave me an opportunity to appreciate more than ever before the countless numbers of people in this country and all over the world, working away in some small or large organisation, or just on their own, for people in need other than themselves.

I had been surprised, not to say startled, at the almost fantastic number of 'happenings' and the overwhelming affectionate messages, arriving in their thousands from all sections of society in this country, from friends and colleagues, unknown refugees and others from all over the world. This friendliness *en masse* suddenly projected to me all at once, was in one way the most tremendous thing that had ever happened to me. But I had mixed feelings, somewhat difficult to define. I asked myself 'How could this be?' Of course it has happened to others, much better known and more worthy, and I would have been too naïve for words not to have anticipated that my closest colleagues would wish to gather round me at such a time. Later when I began to plan a new way of life I found myself preoccupied with two considerations. The first was personal. How had I got into all this and why had I felt a burning compulsion to go on?

I was born in Sunderland, County Durham. My

mother was pretty, hard-working but somewhat scatty, which sometimes rebounded on her tragically. My father, an estate agent by trade, was twice her age and drank whisky like water. I have one sister three and a half years younger than I, and inevitably we were poor. We were respectably Wesleyan Methodist, at any rate on my mother's side, and while I was nine or ten when my father died, I remember nothing about the actual funeral, but I expect the Methodist Minister officiated. My guess is that my father had little time for religion and never went to church but probably was originally Church of England. I remember sometimes hearing him recite large chunks of the Old Testament when he was drunk in somewhat derisory but grand tones. He had a robust sense of humour and made me laugh and he also had a passion for chess and draughts, which he played with the odd crony from time to time, while we were bidden to silence. There were always draughtboards with half-played games about the house and a terrific shindy arose if one of us disturbed the chequers.

My father had been married before and had one daughter older than my mother. She was married and lived in Scotland and we sometimes went there for holidays. His relations, some reputed to have come from Ireland, were all dead, but they are all shrouded in obscurity. He read books and, if I remember rightly, enjoyed light and rather sentimental music. He was an ardent liberal and I recall the large framed photographs of Gladstone above the living-room fireplace, which he proudly enlarged upon to his many friends. What with the age problem, the whisky and what was called in those days 'our station in life'—now I suppose 'petit bourgeois' —although 'petit' is not quite right, mother went through some desperate years following his death. Sometimes her rather charming and scatty optimism helped;

sometimes it did not. We were perpetually moving about, which meant change of schools, friends and everything. Often it was unnecessary but my mother always thought it the best thing to do. Eventually she settled in a little house not far from my sister, then married, but she was knocked down by a car and was in hospital for some years under permanent care until she died in 1945. Once when visiting her she recognised me, only fleetingly, but was as charming and scatty as ever with the nurses.

My mother's family came from Stanhope, a delightful small town at the foot of the moors in the beautiful Durham dales. Not long ago I was driven there and except for modern amenities, there seemed to be little change. On the surface the population apparently remained steady, the annual Stanhope Fair goes on, and the 'gentry' arrive on the twelfth for grouse shooting. My grandfather was the manager of the slate quarries and was called Smurthwaite. The spelling is important and not to be confused with Smirthwaite, which was more Yorkshire than Durham. This name indicates a sort of tribe, within which could be found its own type of talent, imagination, rigidity, cruelty, a definite culture and here and there an obnoxious internal snobbery. None of us have been freed from those love–hate shackles that encumbered the sometimes over-protected members of it. I see it sometimes in my nephews but they are preserved from having suffered from it in its primitive form.

My grandfather and his family lived in a then superior terrace, the houses were built of stone from the quarries, were a good size and had lovely views from all the windows. They were called villas. He was a Wesleyan Methodist local preacher and he used to drive off on a Sunday morning in his pony and trap to preach in the village chapels. He often took one of the daughters with him and discussed the sermon *en route*. They all sang in the choir and travelled outside to take part in or listen to *The Messiah* and other similar musical events.

There were fourteen children born to them, but only seven—three sons and four daughters—survived. As a small child I remember seven small memorial pictures with black frames hanging about in whatever house we lived. The names, birth and death dates of each dead baby were beautifully embroidered, apparently by my mother, and I suppose they came into her possession because she had made them. They were a source of great interest to me. Four of the survivors married spouses from the North-East, one uncle and one aunt did not marry, but alas my father was born within the sound of the big Bow Bell. He was a sort of mixed cockney. It was considered disastrous that my mother had married a man twice her age, that he drank and that he was not a sanctimonious pillar of the Wesleyan Methodist Church, and that he came from London. In any case, my mother, in spite of her church and respectable conformities, had been frivolous and had enjoyed life too much for safety. We were second-class tribesmen. But by far the most dividing line between them and us was that they were pure North-East country stock, dalesmen with the right name and an unbroken culture. This was distinctly obvious on family occasions, and there was a hidden chilly atmosphere, noticeable whenever any discussions of a faintly radical nature took place about things that mattered. This persisted until well on into the lives of various cousins, but it faded as many of them moved away and the North in general softened its attitude to life.

Two of the Smurthwaite women and one of the wives were teachers, the men, in a limited way, did not do too badly in banking, insurance and local government. My mother was at a dame school where she learnt to do exquisite needlework, embroidery and refined cookery, as well as general subjects. This was in some ways more limited in scope than the background of the teachers, but it served her well when times were bad. She tried hard to teach me to sew, embroider and to do complicated knitting. But I was hopeless and remain so, and she always got cross as the work got soaked with my tears. Needless to say, my sister was excellent.

The teaching women were so fearsome that those of the family in my generation and some of the younger ones, even now, when we are being really beastly to ourselves or others, or being boringly dogmatic, murmur: 'O Lord, the Smurthwaites won't lie down.'

My grandmother was much beloved by all and she showed few signs of having borne so many children or having been dominated by a strong man. Like all the Smurthwaites she had fine hair, a rosy complexion and grey-blue eyes. Her daughters were better looking than she, and the last of them, who died in 1968, was a beauty in every way and even at ninety there were distinct traces of her former glory. She was a most difficult woman but men liked her and her wedding photographs are beautiful period pieces. My grandmother was not matriarchal in the sense that her husband was patriarchal, but she was kind. She secretly helped my mother and sent us little luxuries and came to see us when times were difficult. I thought of her when I stole food to give to starving and freezing children in Germany in 1946.

The family, with the exception of my mother, were, of course, rigidly teetotal and among the many offices held by my grandmother in the Church was the Chairmanship of the Durham County White Ribboners, which was a popular temperance movement of the time. They wore little white enamel brooches in the shape of a bow. She was fiercely loyal to Methodism and had no truck with the Church of England. I remembered her when, as an adult, I walked up the aisle in the crypt of St. Paul's to be confirmed.

When my grandmother was sixty she died of cancer of the breast, which the doctor and the family attributed to a blow. Later, when tribal feelings ran high, they said quite scandalously that they wouldn't be surprised if the blow had not been delivered by my grandfather. My mother took me to Stanhope to see her just before she died and I remember it vividly. I had not been told that she was dying but in any case I hardly knew anything about death and as she talked to me gently and told me to be a good girl, I knew without understanding that she faced death with equanimity. My grandfather lived a long time after that, but enraged the tribe because he sold the house, bought a cottage and married his house-keeper. If that was not enough, he not only left her the cottage to live in and some money but also kept all the others waiting until she died, which was years later.

Looking back I know why I became a 'Jack of all Trades', albeit a professional one in the proper and philosophical meaning of the word. When we were young my sister applied herself in detail and concentration to everything she did while I concentrated only on the things that interested me. Even in those I took short cuts, relying on my imagination and wits. In consequence she passed examinations and I, except in drama, reading and English, did not and did not care. I must have driven her crazy because she was always punctual and I was always late. I was keen on music and in my last terms at a school in Sunderland a mistress introduced me to litera-ture in a big way, for which I have always been eternally grateful. I was already reading everything I could lay my hands on and had read most of Dickens before I was ten years old. They were yellow paperbacks and cost about fourpence each; I laughed aloud and wept over them, and I read the *Tale of Two Cities* three times. This was when I ought to have been doing sums and all manner of other things. I fell in love with poetry and was always forcing my sister and my favourite cousin to listen to me reading Tennyson, Browning, Keats and others, as well as long poetical passages from the Bible. They must have been bored to tears. There was no discipline about this but it was most enjoyable.

I produced my first play when I was thirteen with twenty-five children in the chapel and the Minister and the whole congregation turned out in force. Mother wasn't quite sure about this, and when the Minister told her I was a gifted and imaginative child she was not impressed and I can fully understand why. On the whole she found me difficult to cope with. I could not possibly have understood the measure of her problems and she found my sister much more satisfactory and more lovable towards her. I can now understand the reason, but after all I was the eldest and so I was often cruel to my sister and even now I wish I did not remember. She eventually went to a teacher-training college and then took a special training for teaching backward children, and except for the first nine years of her married life has taught ever since.

Finally, when I was fifteen or so my mother, for all the best reasons, thought it a good thing that I should go and live with the unmarried Smurthwaite aunt in Bishop Auckland. She must have been so desperate to get me disciplined and to provide me with some kind of background for the future. At that time I thought it all wrong, but looking back it was to lead me to a greater understanding of people. I disliked my aunt thoroughly and fought her the whole seven years I was with her. Everyone in our circle and in the Church knew about me and my aunt. She lived in a five-roomed, rather dull house and while looking quite attractive and wearing nice clothes, she ran it and me in the classic Victorian fashion then almost over. When she was sixty and a year or so after I left her she met an old friend, a widower, and they married. This caused quite a sensation. Long before she died I felt tremendous compassion for her but I wished I had felt this in the days when I lived with her.

I went to various courses at the local Technical School and then took a job, in the teeth of opposition because I spent most of the money I earned on going weekly to Durham to take lessons in drama and elocution with the wife of the leading tenor in Durham Cathedral Choir, who had a small private drama school. I joined the local amateur operatic society and became the 'favourite' of the professional producer from Darlington; he taught me a great deal about production. I also joined the Choral Society for one year in order to learn *The Messiah*. The conductor was the organist at Durham Cathedral and Elgar came to conduct the concert. I was thrilled.

My two 'debaucheries' during the First World War when I was fifteen and which earned my aunt's approval, were membership of the Band of Hope and the Girl Guides, both attached to the church. I met boys at the Band of Hope, one a first-class musician who haunted my sleepless nights. I signed the pledge every month for a year and regularly recited poems at the meetings. I was a patrol leader in the Guides and there I learned the rudiments of organisation and administration as well as a dim understanding that professionalism was essential if one was to appreciate the arts and that self-discipline was needed for leadership. With my patrol I produced a play made up of extracts from Milton's *Comus*, much to the amusement of the adults who came to see it; I also organised the refreshments, which included ginger wine and scones.

I was in with the 'intellectuals' in our rather snooty
Wesleyan Church and as well as declaring we were
pagans, which made my aunt furious, we also acted and
made music. I earned some money in a concert party
which had in it one or two 'pros' and we travelled around
the pit villages giving shows. My aunt refused to attend
anything in which I took part but she was once present at
a church 'do' when I played Bottom in a much too
'clever' Shakespearian parody. She was horrified. The
Minister, who with his wife was interested in the arts,
tried to explain to my aunt that all my activities were
really respectable, but to no avail. She told him that my
grandmother must be turning over in her grave.

Later I went to work with a remarkable man who was
a religious agnostic, a keen Socialist and a close friend of
Hugh Dalton. He took or sent me all over the pit villages
in relation to his business. This opened out a new world
to me and introduced me to politics. It was in the thirties
and I came to know the Durham miners very well. I
would sit in a miner's kitchen and talk books and politics
while he bathed in the tin tub in front of the fire. I saw
poverty in the raw while the 1926 strike proceeded its
miserable way. I was shattered and drama did not seem
to matter any more. Naturally my aunt did not approve
of the new friends, and anyway we were Wesleyan and
they were Primitive Methodists. Our relationship became
impossible and the only release was when I went occa-
sionally to see my mother and sister. I just had to get
out.

I applied and was given a chance to go as a trainee to
the Kendal Y.W.C.A. to learn to be a Youth Leader. The
change was emotionally catastrophic but wonderful. I
built up a sizeable membership in the Club, did drama
all over the place, joined a Shakespearian class run by an
eccentric old Bensonian, climbed the mountains, was

introduced by the Y.W.C.A. to theology which has enriched me ever since, and left five or six years later an entirely different person, having acquired a great love for the Lake District and some lifelong friends.

In 1931 I left Kendal with great reluctance and went to Dagenham, the vast housing estate in Essex, and stayed there until 1945. So different from Kendal. The whole population, over two hundred thousand, were artisans and unskilled workers who had been uprooted from their beloved and much overcrowded East End of London. The ninety miles of streets all looked alike, even their little gardens seemed in the mass to be uniform. The average rent was thirty shillings a week and the average income three pounds ten shillings. To qualify for a house they had to have children and to have lived within the London County Council area. In consequence, for many years Dagenham contained the largest 'under fourteen' population in the British Isles. Two days before the Second World War started we evacuated over twenty thousand children, the largest number to be moved from one town. In the early years all the men and the young people had to travel to London to work. It was not until the war started that they were recruited by Fords and the two related motor organisations, because when they built their massive plant on the Thames-side they brought their workers from other factories which had closed down and they mostly lived in Ilford and Romford.

I was the General Secretary of a large Community Centre and other clubs under the auspices of the Y.W.C.A., later also the Y.M.C.A., the Boys and Girls Clubs Associations and the National Council of Social Service. It was a most exciting and exhilarating experience. I was joined by an old friend to share the leadership and at its height before the war we had a membership of one thousand in a building erected for two hundred. There were programmes for all ages, men and women, adolescents, children and a large staff. Everything we did was a new departure and there were experiments galore. People came to see us from all over the world. We were also pioneering mixed clubs and were reputed to be wild and somewhat 'permissive'. We were democratic to an almost unreal and obsessive degree. As well as the large administrative responsibility there were opportunities for developing drama, music, sport and every kind of social and community development. There were also really difficult family problems, natural in a community of uprooted people. The war changed everything, we had innumerable air-raids and were also involved with refugees who had come to Britain from Germany and other European countries.

Everything I had done and pursued previously had set the stage for me. The family background, the battles with my aunt, my own emotional experiences, the developing interest in the arts—especially the theatre—and the political and theological insights I had acquired, had prepared me in a way that no formal and narrow training would have done. We had to handle large numbers of people, conceive large programmes calling for professional attitudes, and there were human problems within a situation which demanded something much more comprehensive and deeper than the general run of social and community development.

During the war I was the drama adviser for the County of Essex Girl Guide Association and did a great deal of drama for the Essex Education Committee, organising drama courses, teaching and producing and adjudicating at drama festivals. After the war I refused various offers to take on full-time drama advising for various educational committees.

I resigned immediately the end of the war was in sight

and by then I had at last acknowledged to myself that while I would always love the theatre, it was not in any way to be my whole life. This was not only because I was too unsure of myself and my ability, or that I had acquired a considerable interest in administration, especially in the realm of ideas, but probably because I lacked the courage to go out into the cold. In any case I had postponed it for too long. I have never regretted the decision.

In January 1946 I went to Germany for the Y.M.C.A. to develop educational programmes for the soldiers who were slowly but surely being demobilised. I am still grateful to the Y.M.C.A. for the chance they gave me, because there I made some decisions about my future and acquired the necessary discipline. It was there I saw suffering beyond description among the German population and in the refugee camps and I knew that sooner or later I must be involved somehow or other in helping to reduce the suffering of so many people and I must be in a position to fight for the right of man to be free wherever he was. But before I was fully occupied in this endeavour I accepted the invitation to be Secretary of the Youth Department of the British Council of Churches. A good deal of the work was involved in youth leadership training, ecumenical education all over the British Isles and bringing together German and British young people. A major activity was encouraging the youth of the churches to be conscious of the needs of the community and the quarter of a million refugees who had come to live in these islands. From there I went to Inter-Church Aid, now Christian Aid and then in its infancy, which is what this book is about. This is how I came into the whole business of aid and the complete involvement with those in need all over the world.

My preoccupation with drama was invaluable to me as Christian Aid developed. It helped me to exercise a 'professional' judgement of scripts and locations when Christian Aid made films, which it did approximately every two years. In 1954 the World Council of Churches held its Second Assembly at Evanston, Illinois, U.S.A., and I was asked to be responsible for the Inter-Church Aid evening session and to use the medium of drama. I wrote a small play-cum-pageant, entitled *By the Waters of Babylon* and produced it with staff and students of North Western University. It was a truly pioneering experience. The older and 'traditional' theologians insisted on 'purity' of script to an absurd degree, and others insisted on including interludes for speakers, even though one of these, a Korean, knew hardly any English which was the prevailing language. The acoustics in large pockets of the auditorium were terrible, the heat was in the nineties and there was an audience of nine thousand. It was a nightmare. The play was published in Great Britain and performed in churches all over the country. I produced it at the Colston Hall, Bristol, on the occasion of the second British ecumenical Youth Conference. We had the help of students from a local drama school and three actors from London. John Hodgkis composed special music for the production and conducted the Goldsborough Orchestra on the night. It was a compliment to all of us that he thought it worth his while and the orchestra travelled back to London overnight in a coach, in order that we did not have to pay the required double fee for overtime.

The Third Assembly of the World Council of Churches was held in New Delhi, India, in 1960. Christian Aid asked Margaret Johns and her husband Ian Dawson Shepherd of Libertas Films to make us a film about the hunger situation in India, starting with a scene at the Assembly. Max Robertson agreed to speak the commentary. The three of them helped me when I was requested, almost at the last minute, to arrange the Inter-Church evening. We made the film in Britain and took it out with us and, with Max Robertson in the chair, included international interviews about refugees and poverty. The following year Libertas made our most important film to date, *The Long March* directed by Patrick Garland. It was in four countries, in colour, and had a most successful première in London and was seen over four years by thousands of people all over the British Isles and in some other countries.

One of the most successful conferences in the life of the World Council of Churches was held in 1966 on Church and Society. For two weeks there were gathered together in Geneva five hundred participants from every continent of whom seventy-five per cent were lay men and women, representing every conceivable profession and occupation. This was the beginning of the determination of the younger elements in the World Council to be compulsorily concerned about development and revolution. There were eight Presidents of the Conference and I was the 'token' female in that distinguished group. I was grateful that Patrick Garland was able, at my suggestion, to write a dramatic script which included poetry and songs about famous historical revolutionaries and protests. It was called *The Rebel* and included scenes about the peasants' revolt and the Irish massacres as well as the Negro rebellion in the United States. Patrick went to Geneva and handled the 'doubtful' theologians perfectly. He produced it with a cast of British actors, some already playing in London theatres and there were two performances on the second Sunday of the Conference. It was received enthusiastically and after the performance the actors mingled with the members of the Conference to the advantage of all concerned.

Developing an organisation like Christian Aid needed

a 'Jack of all Trades' and I think I was around at the right psychological moment to do a job that needed ideas and imagination as well as organisational capacities. I certainly knew how to take crisis after crisis in my stride. But I believe my most useful contribution to the ecumenical movement in the realm of the arts was that I helped to pave the way in the World Council of Churches for the use of the theatre and films as a necessary adjunct to all major gatherings. The result was that at the Fourth Assembly held at Uppsala in 1968 there were happenings splendidly executed by famous international film-makers, dramatic producers, artists and musicians and while there were predictable 'unnecessary' problems, they did not involve 'stuffiness' and theological eccentricities.

MOTIVES

I was acutely conscious of all that had gone before during the Christian Aid farewell 'dos' when kindness and love were showered upon me. But it was a relief to realise that I had never once consciously thought that I personally had done anything for anybody. This was not a question of pride or false modesty but when I am interested in anything I unconsciously apply the whole of my energy and thought to that end. I was a catalyst and a 'middleman' and that was the function that I had had the privilege to perform. This is surely the occupation of a 'Jack of all Trades' and I had been in a position to communicate to a considerable number of ordinary people that millions of people at home and all over the world were in desperate need. It was really they who had done the work.

During the last twenty years or so 'Charity' has become streamlined big business. This applies primarily to the large organisations and particularly those related to overseas aid, who have to convey to ordinary people the necessity for the rich nations to help the poor nations. The experience gained at the time of major appeals for refugees and war victims in the 1940s, when considerable funds were collected, made it imperative not only that the administration of these funds should be efficiently handled and spent to the best advantage but also the whole process of publicity and education had to be streamlined and professional. In all this I was greatly helped by Hugh Samson, the Public Relations Adviser for Christian Aid. It was a splendid partnership.

I shall be for ever grateful that my time with Christian Aid and working for the ecumenical movement allowed me to travel regularly all over the world. I visited Africa fifteen times and have a great love for many Africans in many countries, seeking to break free of their past problems. But as I say that I remember all the other countries and continents that I have been to on many occasions and the preparation it gave me for the work I am doing temporarily for the Family Welfare Association in London.

My only regret is that the Churches do not use more women and that too often I was the first or the only woman performing some function.

Since I retired from Christian Aid my old friend Alan Brash, who succeeded me, has been most successful in all the developments. Christian Aid is larger and better than ever and the political and educational programmes are most forward-looking and project the proper image for a Christian organisation concerned with aid and development. But without the continuing process of keeping alive a large organisation, Christian or otherwise, concerned with the actual 'giving of the cup of water'—

which means raising money—there would be no point in developing educational and political action.

The individual sentimentalist is still with us even in the Church. If it is true, as I believe, that unity is of the foremost importance, then surely united action for the hungry world is an essential manifestation of the teachings of Jesus. The sentimentalists are generally speaking to be found in greater numbers outside the Church and it really is a form of arrogance and egoism that to me is intolerable. Whenever anyone says to me 'but you see, I love people', I shudder. It is manifestly untrue or at best, superficial. It usually means an attitude of paternalism or a form of therapy for overwrought men and women. I feel compelled to support those who are struggling to ensure that people of all sorts get what is their right and that they are treated with compassion and love. 'I love people' rarely means that, although in any one day of my life the most exciting thing that can happen is to meet someone alive and interesting who either inflates my mind or enriches my spirit: it is a sad truth that most of us do not 'love people' but just the reverse.

The second consideration, still with me, was the motive. Was it Christian? I do not know. Something had to be done and I did it without considering why. When asked by Christopher Chataway on a television programme whether I had felt called by God to be compelled to do compassionate work for those in need, I said 'No, not that I am aware of' because I had never understood what that question meant. I was criticised for giving that answer, and in reply I asked whether my critics would rather I had told a lie.

I think I can claim to be a religious person at least in thought if not in deed, and I am an almost fanatical believer in the ecumenical movement in the deepest meaning of the word. The world desperately needs unity.

I believe that Jesus taught the love for mankind that knows no bounds and that the Church or its equivalent is an essential body in any country. It is a necessity in our culture and part of our history even if it is not any more accepted as an essential of life by the majority of the population. I have always found the dogmas and generally accepted doctrines of the Church difficult to accept and mostly impossible to believe. But, even when I have felt isolated and most bored by the Church, I have never been able to dissociate myself from religion and the quest for truth and the meaning of life. Who could not believe in the humanity of Jesus and all that he taught about love and peace? That the Church has allowed me to be its servant, to expound what I think the teaching of Jesus demands for suffering man and has given me its protection in spite of this, has never failed to move me to the depths. I go all the way with the much-quoted sentence from a book by Bertrand Russell at the time of his death: 'Remember your humanity and forget the rest. If you can do so, the way lies open to a new paradise: if you cannot, nothing lies before you but universal death.'

It is ironic that as the quest for unity goes forward the Church and the official ecumenical organisations become more institutionalised and so often irrelevant in this day and age. The language, the narrowness of those obsessed with institutional affairs, the fear that prevents leaders being honest about their doubts and the growing gap between ordinary people and the Church is tragic. But if man has to die to have lived, then I suppose the Church must do the same. What is unchanging is that others within and without the Church as well as I are in pursuit of truth and the less they believe the more they need the love and freedom that Jesus taught. This compulsion is of course to be found in other cultures and religions and among humanists. Their adherents face the same dilemmas.

How can I escape, but how can any of us assess our motives for what we do? I do not know. But a significant feature of society today is the fact that the Churches together have done, and are doing, more for suffering humanity than almost any other institution and this is true to their calling. But even more significant is the increasing compulsion of ordinary men and women, including young people, living in an increasingly sophisticated world, who while unable to accept the Christian faith in a 'package deal' or as a philosophy of life, are in large numbers occupied with caring for the refugees, the persecuted, the homeless and all in need. If it is true that God is everywhere whether we are there or not, or believe it or not, then whether their motives are Christian or not is of secondary importance. What to me is of primary importance is that I should continue the search, and refute with all the power and anger that I can muster, the inhuman barriers raised between man and man whatever the cause, different backgrounds of class, pseudo-intellectualism, religion, the colour of a man's skin, the ease with which nations resort to war, or the inhumanity of man caused by selfishness and the pursuit of power.

Sydney Carter wrote a poem called 'The Miracle':

> *Tight as a headache*
> *the congested crags*
> *hem in the traveller*
>
> *but suddenly*
> *the humped obsession cracks*
> *and clapping waves*
> *cry alleluia.*

With my fingers cupped
I kneel again
by the forgotten lake,
lifting infinity.

2

REFUGEES—A PERMANENT OBLIGATION

REFUGEES—A PERMANENT OBLIGATION

Dreamed I saw a building with a thousand floors,
A thousand windows and a thousand doors,
Not one of them was ours, my dear, not one of
*   them was ours.*
              From 'Refugee Blues' by W. H. Auden

'BENGAL REFUGEE SERVICE cordially invites you to the official opening of the first house in the Sealdah Refugee Re-settlement, Garshyannager, India, on Wednesday, 1st April 1964.' How I wished I could have accepted that invitation. On my way home from Thailand a few months earlier I had seen that house being built in a refugee colony on the outskirts of Calcutta. An Indian woman with her baby in her arms stood patiently watching her husband and other men putting the roof on a small house. We would call it a shack. She turned and took hold of my hand and asked the interpreter to tell me that this was the happiest day of her life. She had never imagined she would ever have a proper home again. She was one of 8,000 refugees from what is now Pakistan, who had lived, if you can use the word, on the platforms and sometimes in the custom sheds of Sealdah, the main railway station in Calcutta. Some of the refugees had been there ever since independence when the partition between India and Pakistan had taken place. That was fifteen years. During the fighting, just after independence, a tremendous number of refugees crossed the new border into India because they had the wrong religion for the new country. Three and a half million of Hindu refugees who had to leave Pakistan settled in West Bengal. There were also a large number of Muslims who crossed the new borders the other way for the same reason. Thousands squatted in the Calcutta railway station and it almost became a tourist 'attraction'. Their homes were a square section roughly 6 feet by 9 feet marked out with ropes, and pathetic bits of rags on four rickety sticks about $4\frac{1}{2}$ feet high were their only cover. I had been there when the heat was very great and the refugees were sullen and definitely hostile. Some years previously the Government had moved a few thousand out of the station but before long others had taken their place.

The Bengal Refugee Service, a project arranged by the National Christian Council of India, decided with the help of Churches throughout the world and the co-operation of the Indian Government, to make an 'all-out' effort to move the refugees to permanent homes. The Bengal Refugee Service found the Government more than ready to co-operate. The Government gave the land for three colonies a few miles outside the city for the permanent resettlement of over ten thousand refugees. The Indian Railways provided a train which would carry a hundred passengers and would be on call to leave at midnight each night as and when required. I was there when the first train took the first hundred. The excitement was electric. Parents and children with their pathetic bundles filed into the train laughing and shouting and I felt with them that a miracle had happened. The refugee service staff and the refugees themselves erected tents on the 'virgin' land and immediately began to build their own houses. Local Indian architects gave their services, planning and supervising the building and using a new Japanese type of brick which the men made themselves. The unemployed were paid the local rate for the job and others with jobs commuted into Calcutta and worked on the site at week-ends. Food was supplied by the Refugee Service. Later seven international medical teams were set up, simple schools were built by arrangement with the Government and small industries developed to provide employment. Trade schools for adolescents were started almost immediately. The Bengal Refugee Service came to an end after six years, with their part of the rehabilitation of the refugees completed. The initial survey was carried out by Church World Service, U.S.A., and funds, as well as staff provided by many ecumenical agencies. Christian Aid in Britain as well as contributing considerable funds out of World Refugee Year money, recruited workers who included an Englishman who supervised the great exodus from Sealdah Station. The Government made sure no more refugees squatted in that station. The medical teams were taken over by various missionary groups and the schools by the Government. Just imagine being on Liverpool Street Station without a roof in a temperature of 112° F. for eight years and then being given a small house of your own in a wooded field with prospects of education and work. No wonder that woman was happy!

TIBETANS

On that same journey I visited for the second time Tibetan refugees at Rajpur and Mussorie, about seven hours' drive from New Delhi, and met over one thousand Tibetan refugees. Mussorie is a hill station where Europeans and more well-to-do Indians go for their holidays in the hot weather. It is mountainous and just the right atmosphere for Tibetans who belong to hill country. There are 35,000 Tibetans in India and 20,000 in Nepal. The Christian Council of India was at that time entirely responsible for the care of all the T.B. cases which were a very high percentage of the community. The Government provided half the cost. This medical programme is running down now as the health of the refugees steadily improves.

Tibetans are an energetic people and were making an enormous effort to make the best of being permanently in exile. They had not recovered and never will from the terrible shock of being overrun by the Chinese, and the nightmare journey across mountains regarded as inaccessible will never be forgotten by any but the babies. Some adults were working on the road breaking stones and looking forward to the provision of a stone-crushing machine by the Welfare Committee of the Christian Council. There were tailors' shops, women weaving blankets, men making tin trunks and many groups working in handicraft shops in near-by villages. The tools were primitive but the people were occupied and earning their keep. The children were given supplementary food.

I spent a happy day in the schools where there were six hundred children of all ages. They were in the care of Mr. and Mrs. Rinchen Dolma Taring, a remarkable couple, relatives of the Dalai Lama. With help from all over the world, mostly from Christian Churches, they had started formal education for the children in buildings loaned to them, set up hostels and opened twenty homes for twenty-five children in each with foster parents. Two of the homes were provided by the British Ockenden Venture, three by a Swiss organisation and several by the Christian Council of India. The Christian Council had just built a small hospital and the English nurse there was provided by the Save the Children Fund. Christian Aid has helped the Tibetans with funds ever since they left Tibet.

Mrs. Taring was making sure that the children were

given a good education and so would be able to earn their living and settle in a strange land. The children are selected by the Dalai Lama who feels the most important activity for young Tibetans in exile is education, but like all refugees they believe that one day they will return to their own country and so they prepare for that day. The project still flourishes.

During the week I was there the Dalai Lama came to open a Buddhist Temple which was for the use of all the Tibetans in that district. The money had been raised by the people themselves and the Temple built with their own hands. I wished all our Christian Aid helpers in the British Isles could visit those schools and see the adult activities in the area. They would have felt a great sense of satisfaction when they saw the progress of such a practical and excellent project.

BORDERS

Every day refugees cross borders somewhere in the world, in fear and hope, in despair and hopelessness, taking a chance of a better future, because they feel rightly or wrongly that nothing could be worse than the life they have left behind. I have stood on such borders all over the world watching police on both sides, sometimes standing on raised platforms, guns at hand, and sometimes just gazing at each other at a distance of ten yards. Sometimes they are of the same race, like those at the Hong Kong border, or between East and West Germany, or in Korea, and more recently in various parts of Africa. I always find it impossible to understand what the refugees are feeling inside themselves as they take such risks, having made a terrible decision to run, rather than to stay. There is nothing romantic about being a refugee.

It is just horrible.

When I saw Hungarians cross over into Austria in 1956, I felt I was watching humanity 'red in tooth and claw'. Some boys were wounded and others were half carrying them. They had literally just left off firing guns and were wounded or battle-scarred. All were humiliated at having to leave their own land which they had hoped to free from tyranny. When ten years ago I saw some of the thousands leaving East Germany for the West, they always looked tight-lipped and apprehensive, as though they were political and spiritual orphans and did not belong anywhere. They were weeks and sometimes months in the vast, tightly packed reception camps before they were 'cleared' and then transported to the Ruhr and various industrial cities in Western Germany. Few cross over now and only by taking terrible risks. Is it worth it? I wonder! Chinese crossing from China into Hong Kong look tidy and inscrutable and somehow seem resigned to a journey with no end in sight. Yugoslavs cross into Austria trying hard to look casual and disinterested, knowing that their need to come out will be questioned. How can the watcher on the right side of the border begin to understand the agony hidden behind the masks which the refugees put on as their only defence against an unknown world? On these occasions it is even more impossible than usual to get inside another person's mind and heart, and so understand his actions and needs. How did they decide what to pack in their one suitcase? Their best clothes? Sometimes they did that only to find that their one suit or dress was quite unsuitable when they found manual jobs. 'Which members of the family can we leave behind in the hope that we shall all be together again later?' is the most agonising decision facing all refugees whether 'economic', 'political', 'war victims' or 'persecuted'.

It is almost impossible for an ordinary British citizen living today to grasp that probably every day and every night since the Lord said to Joseph in a dream 'Get up now and cross the border into Egypt', families have been crossing borders into foreign lands because of fear or persecution, most of them knowing they would never return. It was no new experience for the relatives and forbears of Jesus to be political or economic refugees. The Old Testament is full of stories of battles, exiled peoples, refugees and the passionate and tragic life stories of men and women struggling to survive. Judah and Israel together formed a corridor between the Mediterranean Sea and the Syrian desert. As well as being in revolt against foreign domination, the people were always engaged in the struggle against drought and famine.

EUROPE

Our own history books are full of wars won and lost. When the Romans occupied Britain, there must have been many who escaped across the sea in little boats to find shelter on remote islands or foreign shores in order to remove themselves as far as possible from the invaders. When despotic kings ruled, inevitably there were men and women who tried to survive by crossing our border, which is the sea. French refugees came to England in the seventeenth century to escape from persecution because they were unwilling to denounce their Protestant faith. The Pilgrim Fathers went to America to find more freedom for their beliefs. Wherever there have been revolutions, people have gone into exile; sometimes they were chiefly aristocrats, sometimes chiefly peasants, but mostly they were all sorts and conditions of men. Very often the bitter passions of exiled people have created situations which resulted in other people becoming refugees.

We look on the problem of refugees and borders as something removed from us; we cannot do much about it anyway. We have our lives to live.

One of my most poignant memories of the Second World War was helping to receive refugees from Belgium. Hitler had just overrun Holland and Belgium and occupied the whole of France. Two hundred Belgian civil servants, who had hurriedly left Brussels with government documents, large sums of money and anything else that they could quickly get together, found themselves in England on the outskirts of London, where I was working at the time. As the Germans approached Brussels, these men had been told to go to a ship which would take them to a secret place in France. Their wives and families were bundled into a train which was to follow them as soon as possible. The ship was bombed incessantly and for safety's sake they crossed the Channel and landed at Folkestone. Their families sat in the train or hid in the woods by the side of the railway line for three days. The train never moved and they eventually went back to their homes, and they neither saw nor heard of their menfolk for five years.

We put the men up in a large hall—ordinary middle-class men, looking what they were, typical well-dressed civil servants, but bewildered and apprehensive. All were worried about their families and quite unable to visualise what the future might hold for them. Like all tragic situations it had its funny side too. We had expected women and children, poor and decrepit, carrying what one might call refugee bundles. Kindly helpers had made up camp beds and put under the pillows flimsy nightdresses. In the panic no-one remembered to move the female attire put there to comfort the women. I learned afterwards that when the men grimly and silently turned back the blankets and found the feminine negligees, they dressed up and danced round and laughed until they wept.

The next day they wept again. We were all gathered together listening to the nine o'clock news on the radio. The announcer said all was quiet in Belgium, the King had been confined to his castle and the country was well and truly occupied. Then Winston Churchill, in never-to-be-forgotten language, told us what had happened to Belgium, Holland and France. We were stunned. Then one man said, 'I've lost my family, my country and my King. As a foreign office official I have sworn to be his servant loyally and devotedly, and I have been loyal to that promise. What is there left to live for now?' We all wept.

This story is illustrative of a scene that has been enacted thousands of times all over Europe and is still going on all over the world. It also shows the illusions we have about refugees. Well-dressed, middle-class men, and not poor peasants. Refugees are all sorts and conditions of men, suddenly uprooted from their homes and a way of life not unlike our own.

To understand the problems of European refugees we must take into account some milestones in European history, when for centuries there has been a continuous stream of people moving from one country to another. Sometimes they have skirted round a blood-drenched battlefield or perhaps escaped from a city which was in the process of being blasted to the ground. Refugees and homeless people are always on the move. Tragically, what happened in Europe is being repeated today in Asia, Africa and Latin America.

When you read about the fall of the Roman Empire, the collapse of the Austrian Empire, the partitioning of nations by conquerors, the civil wars in Spain and Ireland, the problems of the Baltic States, the French and Russian revolutions, you can be certain that there were helpless people crossing borders either secretly or by force, becoming wanderers in a no-man's land of obscure suffering. Today Europe is probably still the most vulnerable continent. It is partly because there are so many overcrowded countries in a small area, with different languages and cultures. Their common tie is the Christian religion but the very nature and division of the Churches in the modern world weakens the reality of their calling to reconcile mankind. During the last fifty-odd years seventy million people in Europe have been rendered homeless or have become refugees because of two world wars and political civil wars—one in eight of the total European population. No wonder many Americans ask why Europe does not unite and become like the United States.

Dr. M. J. Bonn wrote:

It must take a long time before the several nations comprised within a European unity can evolve a common European patriotism which will keep them united after external pressure has gone. For over a thousand years they have opposed universalism. Their history is a history of revolt against it. They broke away from the all-embracing Holy Roman Empire. They rose in the Reformation against the strongest universalist system heretofore known. Nationalism, that brain-child of Europe, is but the positive assertion of her people's hatred of uniformity and universalism.

Great Britain is geographically in Europe and must increasingly be part of the economy and within the economic atmosphere of Europe. But many British people, in spite of the thousands who cross the channel every year with package tours, think of the continent as 'foreign' and their attitude is one of aloofness. This has something to do with language and basic theological differences. While not many people in any country would believe that theology has anything to do with modern attitudes and decisions, for centuries cultures continued to be influenced by a basic theological habit pattern of life without being aware of it. This background has, I am sure, something to do with an unconscious resistance by many British people to joining the European Common Market. We will have to change our attitude but my guess is that it will be out of necessity rather than whole-sale choice. The ties with some Commonwealth countries and the United States are closer in language and culture, and generally speaking we are in Europe and not of it. When we are generous with our money and receive re-fugees hospitably when they come, as they did at the time of the Hungarian revolution, we utterly fail to understand that what has happened to these people could and might happen to us, and that they are the wounded from a common front line in the battle for freedom, which is no new battle but has been a continuous one for centuries.

Many have been refugees more than once. There are refugees in this country who have been in five or six countries of asylum and lived in as many as twenty to twenty-five camps since the Russian revolution in 1917. Now those old refugees, finally settled in Britain or some other country, wait to die among the 'hard core', the last remaining group of 'ultimate' refugees.

In a poem 'Refugee Blues', W. H. Auden wrote:

Thought I heard the thunder rumbling in the sky;
It was Hitler over Europe, saying, 'They must die';
O we are in his mind, my dear, O we are in his mind.

GERMAN REFUGEES IN GERMANY

One of the great problems at the end of any war is to decide where armistice lines should go, and to share out the conquered land and agree the terms of occupation. After the Second World War the Allies, that is the United States of America, France, the U.S.S.R. and the United Kingdom, had to agree to make new boundaries. This again, as always, meant expelling people *en masse* from their homelands, and millions of people were deported from eastern German states taken over by Poland and Russia. They came in their thousands from Silesia, Pomerania, East Prussia and other areas.

I was working in Germany in 1946 and saw the arrival in Hanover and Hamburg of thousands of these people in the worst European winter in living memory. They arrived in goods trains, many died on the way or were so frost-bitten that their physical condition was pitiable to see. Schleswig-Holstein, with a population of one million, within a short space of time had two million, and as its main cities were bombed to the ground accommodation was indescribably bad. As in all refugee emergencies, they were seeking only bed-space. In fact, since the last war Germany, both East and West, has absorbed over thirteen million of these expellees, most of them ethnic Germans. It is impossible to assess what happened to the hearts and minds of the people involved in this mass exile, even if they are still in another part of their own country. Their culture and habits are different, they are dubbed 'refugees' and they feel lost in an atmosphere of humiliation and loneliness. Until the wall was built in Berlin in 1961 nearly four million refugees had crossed over from the East of Germany to the West.

WHY DO THEY LEAVE HOME?

In 'totalitarian' states, whatever the basic political philosophy, there are pressures brought to bear upon the citizens that are outside our understanding. The pattern of life with its accompanying pressure is similar wherever it is, in any part of the world. For example, young people are constantly being pressed to join political youth groups. Slogans are repeated hour by hour on radio and in the cinema. Worst of all, when the propaganda is ignored by these young people, certain privileges are withheld. These privileges are the ordinary necessities of a young person's life: membership of a sports club, a place in the football team and the use of the swimming pool. Those young people who act against their elders' advice and join the political youth organisations are often encouraged to spy on their parents and relatives and to report about their attitude to the State.

The effect of social and economic pressure on a family can be devastating. I have written elsewhere about a family who lived a simple life on a small farm which had been theirs for generations, taking their full share in the life of the community and the local church. In addition to what he feared would happen to the personalities of his children, the farmer had day by day, month by month, worries that kept him tossing sleeplessly on his bed at night. He felt as though the cold tap was dripping on to his forehead incessantly and slowly sending him mad. He did not understand what was happening. Some said his fears were groundless, but whether they were or not, the atmosphere got the better of him. The State demanded that he should grow a certain quota of potatoes. From the first the quota was higher than his land could yield, and then it went up every year. Droughts or pests or sickness were ignored, and he feared prison, the loss of his home and land, or worse. Then one night he cried, 'I can't bear this any longer. We must go.' A terrible decision, because he knew there was no return. If they were caught while escaping, they were doomed to persecution, or they might find death from hidden mines on the frontier; if they crossed the frontier safely, they were joining the queue of refugees with its long years of waiting, its life in camps, and for an unknown period life would be indescribably dreary. Many people in his former country would say he need not have left, but he did.

They packed two suitcases—deciding what to put in the suitcases was a major problem—and set off to cross to the West. Then they had to produce a good reason for being refugees: they found that the West was not a heavenly place with the streets paved with gold, and their whole faith and attitude to life was put to a drastic test that went on and on. Now they are resettled, but the scars will remain as long as they live.

There are thousands of families in similar predicaments. You might say, that is 'old hat', twenty years old, but it is happening today, although the conditions and climates in Africa, Asia and Latin America are different, and could happen again in Europe. The story of Christian Aid must record what the Churches did in those years after the Second World War, and why, if we are to understand what we might have to do some time in the future.

DISPLACED PERSONS

Young people today have hardly ever heard of the concentration camps found all over Germany at the end of the Second World War, or of the horrifying and diabolical cruelty meted out to millions of men and women just because they were Jews. Every kind of torture was used on them, the like of which we have only read in descriptions of torture in the dark ages or have conjured up in our minds when looking at instruments of torture in the Tower of London. They were starved of food and lived under indescribable conditions, with their prison numbers branded on their arms and bodies with red-hot irons. They had to 'line up' to await their turn for the gas chambers. There were millions more who were not Jews but were in countries other than their own at the end of the war and unable to return because of changing political policies and borders. They were called Displaced Persons. Young people today quite rightly think that we must face the human problems of today and forget the past. But no history of the Churches' care for rejected and homeless people would be complete without recalling the years in the thirties and forties when so many men and women endured indescribable suffering. From the beginning and to the end of this prolonged crisis the Churches together were there to help and rescue them.

Whenever there is a mass movement of refugees, there are large numbers of children, often moving in groups or alone. There is nothing more tragic to gaze upon than one child dragging its feet, alone and yet determined to arrive somewhere. Children who survive such dreadful experiences have managed to do so because they have had to adjust themselves to unnatural and dangerous circumstances and tremendous hazards.

I saw and tried to talk to some of these children in large underground, dimly-lit bunkers in Hanover in 1945 and 1946. Some had been walking, mostly at night, for two years from one side of Germany to the other. They lived like animals and their faces were like those of old men and women of eighty. The social workers living in the bunkers had to stay below in the dark because the children were afraid of the light. What, I wonder, are they like today? How many children today are wandering on other continents because of cruel wars and persecution, and what can be done about it?

After release from concentration or labour camps in 1945 the nine million 'foreigners' were transferred to displaced persons' camps hurriedly prepared by the United Nations Relief and Rehabilitation Administration (U.N.R.R.A.). Six million or so were people from Poland, Estonia, Lithuania, Latvia and the Ukraine. Mostly they were slave labourers brought by the Nazis to Germany to help in the war effort. Some were from the German-occupied countries and were quickly sent home. The majority of those who did not return to their own countries were emigrated or economically settled in Germany and other nearby countries. Ninety per cent of the two million displaced persons in Europe who emigrated to the United States, Australia, Canada and other countries, were sponsored and cared for by churches of all denominations, who were helping U.N.R.R.A. in its colossal task. A quarter of a million of these stateless people came to the United Kingdom.

After U.N.R.R.A. came a number of United Nations organisations and finally the International Refugee Organisation which closed in 1951. The World Council of Churches had from the beginning been asked to help the United Nations agencies, sometimes in relief teams but to a great extent by finding sponsors in immigrant countries when refugees were accepted for resettlement. The United National High Commissioner for Refugees was appointed in 1951, but unlike the previous bodies his office had and still has no operational powers. Since 1951

the World Council of Churches, the National Catholic
Welfare Council, the Lutheran World Service and the
Jewish agencies have been the major official bodies with
professional staff who operated under contract to the
High Commissioner for Resettlement Programme. In the
main resettlement in this connection was emigration. The
U.N.H.C.R. is one of the most valuable and helpful of
the United Nations' specialised agencies and although it
never has enough money, large numbers of refugees all
over the world have been helped by it.

FLIGHT AND RESETTLEMENT

In 1955 U.N.E.S.C.O. published a book with this title
providing a record of what was observed and accomplished in the management of the grim problems of displaced persons since the end of the war in 1945. There
were twelve contributors including Dr. Maud Bülbring
who was the World Council of Churches Resettlement
Officer working with Christian Aid in London until she
died in 1960.

She wrote about the receiving community in Great
Britain:

It has become customary to measure the share
which receiving countries have taken in the solution of
the post-war refugee problem by the numbers of displaced persons whom they have accepted from the
D.P. camps in central Europe. By this standard Britain's share is small, merely 87,000 refugees for a
population of almost 50 million. But Britain had in
addition offered a new home to the 200,000 members
of the Polish forces under British command, of whom
130,000 accepted that offer; and later she took a fur-

ther 1,300 so-called 'hard core' D.P.s; so that in all the numbers resettling in Britain amounted to over 200,000 since the war. If in addition we bear in mind that Britain gave shelter to several hundred thousand refugees before and during the war, many of whom remained when the war was over, then we may accept the official estimate of about 400,000 refugees resettling or freshly resettled in Britain today.

ETHNIC REFUGEES

An 'Ethnic' refugee is a person of one origin, say Greek, who was born in Albania, lived in a Greek community, spoke Greek, ate Greek food and attended the Greek Orthodox Church. But while remaining Greek, with an accent half-Greek and half-Albanian and born and bred in Albania, when thrown out of Albania and put into a refugee camp in Greece he is as foreign there as he was in Albania. He belongs nowhere. He is the last in the line for resettlement because he has no refugee status.

In recent times in Europe they were Volksdeutsche in Germany and Austria and not recognised by the United Nations as refugees. They had been born in the Sudetenland in Czechoslovakia and over the generations they had retained their own religion and culture, in Greece they were from Albania and other bordering countries, they did not belong anywhere and had two cultures and two languages. When the Nazis came to Czechoslovakia they cleared the Sudetenland of 'Germans'. Those who survived and turned up in camps in Germany were neither Czech nor German, they were abandoned and in the beginning only the Churches helped them. I have met ethnic British in many parts of the world and they helped me to understand the problems of ethnic refugees; I think ethnic displaced persons are perhaps the most tragic and pathetic refugee classification. Generally, refugees and displaced persons reoccupied old prisoner-of-war camps and when they emigrated or were resettled locally the ethnic refugees took over the decrepit barrack huts.

Refugee camps, wherever they are, have a peculiar smell, a mixture of dirt, rats and the human smell of underfed people living in cramped conditions. In a refugee camp or a large dormitory building in some remote field where all kinds of families and individuals are herded together, they and everything around them are mixed up and confused. Family problems are tragically acute and last a long time. They come from different cultures, they have different languages and dialects and they eat different food. When you are displaced, all these things assume great importance. Eating your own type of food, even if previously you had been half starved, is the beginning of a return to security. Communication is often difficult and barriers are created that are hard to tear down. The most difficult problem for the emigrated, especially the aged, is language. Many refugees become mentally sick as they get older, some younger refugees need special treatment from time to time and such treatment must be administered by someone who speaks the same language; such a person is not always easy to find. This is still a problem in this country as some of our refugees are now old and have never mastered English.

It is hard enough for any of us especially if we live in towns to know how one's neighbours live and what their home life is like. We know by sight the people in the ground floor flat next door—sometimes we exchange greetings as we come in and out, we have gossiped on and off for five years with the people three doors away, they seem nice, once they came to tea, but we know nothing about them or how they live. How must refugees, now elderly even after all these years and speaking little English, closed in on themselves, feel about the lack of communication? The result of these problems is a high figure of suicide and mental illness. Housing is always a major problem for refugees, displaced persons and immigrants in any country or continent anywhere in the world.

RESIGNATION AND CHAOS

W. H. Auden in 'Refugee Blues', wrote:

> *Say this city has ten million souls*
> *Some are living in mansions, some are living in*
>   *holes,*
> *Yet there's no place for us, my dear, yet there's no*
>   *place for us*

I remember moving about in Hong Kong for some weeks among a million or more refugees and destitute people, many living in shacks made of cardboard. There was an old woman of eighty-three living alone on a hillside in a little hut made of disintegrating thin tar paper, useless in the wind and rain. A neighbour said, 'This hut will never stand another typhoon.' The old woman replied, 'Never mind, let it collapse and bring me with it.'

Jesus knew all about being homeless. 'The foxes have holes and the birds of the air have nests but the son of man hath not where to lay his head.' He chose to leave his home in order to be with the poor and the most ordinary of us all. If he returned today he would be among the refugees; he and his family were refugees. He would probably be treated as a second-class citizen by many of us, even some of us protesting about human rights and leading world poverty campaigns. He would come from the same overcrowded stinking huts, and project the smell that would be offensive to us in our modern clinical society. He would be difficult. The only right remaining for most refugees is to be difficult. Some of the awkwardness displayed by 'personalities' in refugee camps is because their rescuers are possessive and socially and politically paternalistic. Only the rare person can overcome refugee apathy and question such attitudes. Inevitably he is classified as ungrateful and a nuisance. He would be wearing the wrong clothes and would *feel* a second-class citizen and only a few would recognise him. He would probably be rejected by the protesting students and marchers because they have their built-in ritual which frequently is without love or humour.

AFRICA AND ASIA

When I visit refugee communities in Africa and Asia I see that the basic human problem is the same as those in Europe. I remember comparing a large camp of young people in Schleswig-Holstein which I used to visit when I worked in Germany in 1946 with one I visited in Tanzania five years ago. The boys and girls, part of one and a half million displaced war victims, had come from Pomerania, Silesia and East Prussia in 1950. They were German but not really wanted. Poles were now living in their homes and they were very bitter. These young people were lying on 'camp' beds rotting their lives away. They were there for a long, long time.

Some years later when visiting the camps outside Dar-es-Salaam in Tanzania, I found a large number of young refugee boys. They came from South Africa, the Sudan and Burundi, all eager to continue their education. But there were no schools available. I instantly thought of those German young people I had come to know twenty years before. The only difference was that the young Africans were eating indifferent bean dishes and the young Germans were eating indifferent stew. It was an agonising experience. What would happen to those African boys? On my return from that African journey I broadcast on the BBC and had a long friendly letter from a woman who said I obviously did not know Africa or my geography, that it was impossible for the refugees to have travelled so far and they had obviously been pulling my leg. In fact I had travelled extensively in Africa, I appreciated distances and I knew they had walked tremendous distances and taken long-drawn-out risks to get asylum. I decided it was useless to explain to her that some of the much younger refugee children I had been with in 1948 in Hanover had walked from the extreme East of Germany to the West. I have met refugees in Austria who had drugged their children, put them in barrels and little carts, and climbed over the higher mountains to cross from their country to the freedom of a barrack hut in the West. Sometimes as they made their last spurt they had died of exposure or were shot to death. The Africans had similar experiences and their plight was the same human tragedy.

THE OLD BELIEVERS

One of the most successful refugee resettlement projects carried out by the World Council of Churches was

creating colonies of Old Believers from Russia in Brazil
and in Argentina. Others went to Australia and New
Zealand. The Old Believers broke away from the Russian
Orthodox Church in the seventeenth century. It was said
that at one time there were over twenty-six million but I
cannot vouch for this figure. They have always lived in
primitive agricultural colonies, moved about in groups of
two hundred and more, dressed, farmed, worshipped and
believed in the same way as when they separated themselves from the Orthodox Church. They were victims of
the 1917 revolution and moved into China only to suffer
the same fate when the Chinese revolution took place.
Many landed up in Hong Kong but were not allowed to
stay there permanently. The major difficulty of emigration possibilities was that they insisted on staying together in their particular groups. It is no easy task to
move over a hundred people to another continent while
they insist on not being separated and demand land for
them to farm co-operatively.

I visited them in Brazil and there they were in villages,
the land provided by the Brazilian Government by
arrangement with the World Council of Churches.
They were still scorning doctors, living to a great age,
farming co-operatively, retaining their ancient dress and
building their little houses as before. Those I visited in
Australia were beginning to break away from the enclosed communities. The World Council resettled over
two thousand of them and it was one of the most successful efforts, taking several years to complete.

HUNGARY AND SUEZ

A Revolt and an Attack

On the afternoon of 29th October 1956 Dr. Edgar Chandler, then the Director of the World Council of Churches Refugee Service, was sitting in his office in Geneva when he had a telephone call from Vienna. It was from Arthur Foster, the Senior World Council of Churches Refugee Officer in Austria, who said in his rich Lancashire voice, 'The balloon's gone up.' For months the refugee camps in Austria had been seething with rumours of a revolution. The hotel bars in Vienna, where professional spies and their 'hangers on' were and still are to be found, were also meeting-places for the international Press Corps and other international representatives, and in twos and threes this 'twilight' community looked mysterious and 'knowing' or were unusually silent, but now all hell was let loose.

The Austrian Government, the United Nations High Commissioner for Refugees and the voluntary organisations, mostly religious, the largest being Roman Catholic relief agencies and the World Council of Churches, were already in the middle of an unprepared battle. The weather was terrible, bitterly cold and there was snow everywhere. For two days the world Press had been full of Hungary and Suez and almost simultaneously with the Hungarian rising, British and French troops attacked Port Said for the abortive battle for the Suez Canal. I was in Geneva on the 31st October at a World Council of Churches Refugee Committee, helping to plan what was to be the largest emergency operation for the World Council and the international related agencies since the major post-war refugee programme had started immediately the cease-fire took place in 1945. That night I was in Janet Thomson's flat in Geneva. She was from Scotland and on the staff of the World's Y.W.C.A. We had both suffered acutely all that day about Suez and found it difficult to look our international friends in the eye. We were humiliated and worried. Where would it all end? Now we had our ears as close as we could to the radio first picking up the world comment on Suez, and heard Mr. Gaitskell's impassioned speech, but it was interspersed with cries of anguish from the Hungarian freedom fighters. They had mistakenly been led to believe from the Voice of America and other Western propaganda that if they rose in revolt, the West would rush to their help. This was, of course, never a possibility, and yet our armies with the French were attacking Egypt. As the Hungarians screamed over the radio 'Come now—we can't last much longer', you could hear shots and explosions. We sat frozen in horror and I at least wanted to tear the radio from its socket with the rage of frustration that there was nothing I could do for these people killing each other.

The next day I went to Vienna. The fighting was still going on in Budapest and thousands of refugees were rushing to the border. Every available church and school building was opened to receive the 'new Hungarians'. Hastily-set-up reception centres were manned by the Government and United Nations staff. Welfare programmes were immediately rushed into operation by the World Council of Churches, staff from ecumenical agencies from various parts of the world were rapidly recruited and hundreds of local volunteers helped. Hospital beds were piled into clinics for those who had been wounded and had managed to cross the border, and there were many with feet and hands frost-bitten.

The border between Hungary and Austria had attracted people of goodwill from almost every West European country. Caravans, mobile canteens, estate cars and a motley collection of vehicles turned up, packed with food and clothing. They were lined up along the border and near a river where they could help the refugees to clear the last few yards into Austria. Christian Aid purchased two mobile canteens through the Church of Scotland and it was stocked by J. Sainsbury Ltd., the provision merchants, and manned in the first six weeks by Alec and Mora Dickson of V.S.O. fame. As the various individual vans ran out of money they departed, but the World Council alone manned the most vital places on the border, by then highly fortified for miles, for some months.

I will never forget the little village inn where crowds of young men between the ages of 15 and 20 were taken as they walked or were carried down the half mile of no-man's land to safety. Covered with blood and dirt and some with a burning light in their eyes called out to tell us what they had done in the rising. One spoke with great joy of how he strangled a Russian soldier and then as he died said, 'I got three.' I just did not know what I would have done if I had had a son, whose last words were of joy because he had killed three other young men.

The Austrian Government, with the help of the United Nations, the voluntary agencies and the Churches, set up every type of reception centre and packed refugees into trains for Germany and other countries.

The emigration programme went on at an unprecedented pace. A fleet of new Britannia aircraft made two trips a day between Vienna and London, taking thousands of refugees who remained in Britain, as well as thousands of others who were put on trains for Liverpool and embarked for Canada.

The 21,500 refugees who went to the United States were registered by the voluntary agencies and were processed at the rate of one thousand a day, from the 10th December 1965 and all arrived in the United States by the end of the month.

Undoubtedly religious organisations handled at least 94 per cent of the emigration processing, thus complementing the work of the official United Nations bodies.

In the meantime Great Britain had taken unprecedented action and lifted all restriction on refugee immigration. Approximately fifteen thousand Hungarians arrived in the United Kingdom between Ocotber 1956 and the end of the year. Five thousand eventually left for Canada. A large proportion were young men and while they had been brought up as communists, their parents had religious affiliations and some of them willingly subscribed to one denomination or another. Two-thirds of those who came to the United Kingdom were Roman Catholic. The remainder were Prostestant and of these about two-thirds were Reformed and one-third Lutheran. In this operation as in all others, the Lutheran World Federation co-operated with the World Council of Churches.

This kind of operation is only possible because the member Churches of the World Council of Churches and the Roman Catholic Church are working together, are organised with trained staff and are supported in planning, finance and workers by Christian Councils such as the British Council of Churches, all over the world. The descriptions of the Hungarian convoys were in my mind many times when in 1968 I was helping to devise a more modern method of getting medicaments into Biafra and Federal Nigeria.

In regard to the Hungarian refugees emergency committees were set up by the British Council for Aid to Refugees which is the co-ordinating committee for refugees in this country. The Government provided facilities, paid its first contribution to the Inter-Governmental Committee for Migration, provided staff and offices for reception and other purposes. The Lord Mayor of London raised a quarter of a million pounds, all of which was spent on the programme in this country. Christian Aid raised nearly £100,000 for the World Council Hungarian appeal which eventually reached nearly £250,000, and in addition large quantities of food, clothing and medicines were sent from all over the world. Our refugee resettlement office in London, which was just about to be closed in the autumn of 1956, was responsible for the documentation of all those going to Canada and the National Catholic Welfare Conference did the transportation. The refugee staff was comprised of Dr. Maud Bülbring and Mrs. Templar who worked part-time. They had shared a very small room in Eaton Gate, the Headquarters of the British Council of Churches. Suddenly the building was full of Hungarians; they flooded the Council room, the basement and were sitting on the stairs. In addition the money was rolling in and the finance department was overwhelmed. The British Council of Churches staff helped Christian Aid most nobly and Christian Aid staff worked literally night and day for weeks; at the end of three months two people, including my secretary, collapsed with exhaustion. We then took on more staff, found additional offices, and when the Board thanked the Christian Aid staff, the General Secretary, the Rev. Kenneth Slack, said that as far as his staff was concerned they were grateful to have had a share in the work of Christian Aid.

The Hungarian Community in this country were magnificent and the Lord Mayor gave Christian Aid

£5,000 to buy a house to be a Protestant Hungarian centre. Pastor Varga and many of his people, all 'old' Hungarian refugees who had been in this country for nine years, were given leave of absence from their work and were a tremendous help to all around. Thousands of local church people and their friends gave unstinted service.

I have described this particular refugee emergency in detail because it is typical of what the World Council of Churches Refugee Service, working with the indigenous Churches and Christian Councils, has been doing in various parts of the world since 1945 until today. Naturally the long-term major refugee operation was from 1945 until 1960 and there are still pockets of hard-core refugees under our care. But while the different national situations varied in administration, major refugee programmes, both in the emergency period and the 'follow up', have taken place in Latin America, in various parts of Asia, including Hong Kong, India/Pakistan, Korea, Vietnam, Indonesia and many other places. The Arab refugees have been a major concern for twenty years and more recently various refugee situations have been helped in Africa.

The significant part of this service is that it really is an ecumenical operation including the refugees, the staff, indigenous and foreign, and the donors. There has always been complete co-operation between the World Council of Churches in Geneva and the Roman Catholic Church. Those of my generation in the field are highly amused at the wonder expressed as people tell us as hot news how they are meeting with Roman Catholics in local Councils of Churches. In the Refugee Service we have been doing this without thinking it especially significant for twenty years; have also regularly exchanged staff and together we have helped non-Christian refugees without any demands for allegiance.

One of the young Hungarian refugee students said on leaving Victoria Station for Canada, 'I still don't believe in God, but I do believe in Dr. Bülbring.'

WORLD REFUGEE YEAR

'Wanted, a World Refugee Year.' This was the title of an article in the April 1958 issue of *Crossbow*. It was written by Christopher Chataway, Colin S. Jones, Trevor Philpott and Timothy Raison—four young politicians deeply disturbed about the fact that, in spite of what the United Nations and the voluntary organisations had done, there were remaining in Europe 200,000 post-war refugees. The majority of them had either lived in decrepit barrack huts or old shacks for at least fourteen years. They were depressed and without hope, some were bitter with deteriorated personalities, bursting out on occasions into ungovernable rage against fate. Some were alcoholics, all were living on charity, and only the children were carefree because camp-life was all they had experienced. They were spoken of as the 'forgotten people' which was only partly true.

The United Nations had not forgotten, although not all the member states contributed to the budget of the High Commissioner for Refugees. The voluntary agencies and the Churches had not forgotten, but the task was too large in spite of the co-operation and co-ordination of all concerned. Governments, once sympathetic, were getting more and more apathetic as the years rolled by, and the refugees got more decrepit and fatalistic.

Undoubtedly the dramatic events of the Hungarian Revolution stirred the consciences of the nations, and the word 'refugee' once again became a tragic world symbol of 'persecution' and at the same time of 'compassion'.

When, during the bitterly cold 1956 winter, frightened Hungarians fled into Austria, crossing the snow-bounded wastes of 'no-man's land', they found waiting for them just within the Austrian border men and women of all nationalities, and were given food and warmth and surrounded with loving care. Within days they were 'documented' and the majority were on the way to countries of second asylum.

We were all thrilled that governments all over the world waived security and 'entry' rules, and within months it was—at any rate on the surface—'refugee operation completed', 'files closed'.

It does not need much imagination to guess what went on in the minds of the 'old' refugees of many nationalities, 'rotting' in the huts and shacks in Austria and Germany as they saw 'new' refugees peering from the windows of trains rushing through stations, speeding their human cargo to new homes and freedom. It was a particularly bitter pill for the 'old' Hungarian refugees to swallow. At first they had felt a new surge of hope. At last it had happened and the iron curtain was rising and they could go home. In a few days their hopes faded. They spent hours with their ears glued to the camp radio sets, and soon their excitement turned to fear as they realised that the revolution had failed, and things for them were as before, hopeless and dreary. We heard of some who sneaked across the border into Hungary and joined the terrified queue re-entering as new refugees. Most were spotted, but I expect a few got away with it. Do you blame them?

The four young Englishmen were speaking for all of us working with refugees when they said. 'There has been a geophysical year, why not a Refugee Year?' And so they lit a torch, and in June 1959 ninety-seven countries rose to the challenge.

SOME FACTS AND FIGURES

Over £30,000,000 was donated, two-thirds from the public and the remainder from governments. This money made it possible to resettle thousands of refugees, to build homes, to burn down the camps and to help refugee families start a new life. Most of the money which poured into the United Nations was in small gifts, some from the poverty-stricken areas of Asia and Africa, and some from old-age pensioners in the United Kingdom. Many countries opened their doors and let in more refugees, and, what is more significant, agreed to receive the aged, the sick and the physically handicapped.

Nearly two thousand came to the United Kingdom and similar numbers went to various Commonwealth countries. After years of waiting, families were reunited because in North America, Australia and many other countries, including Great Britain, strict entry laws were relaxed. Homes for the aged refugees were established in countries all over the world. The World Council of Churches was one of the major international agencies involved in all these programmes. Thirty-four World Council Aged Refugee Homes were opened in Europe, and large contracts were entered into with the United Nations for the purpose of building more homes, making furniture, supporting recreational training centres and providing places of worship for the various religious groups. Many more social workers were recruited, and 'after-care' was provided for the refugees settled in new homes near the camps or in new countries, very often on the other side of the world.

One of the hazards of being a refugee, even after resettlement, is mental illness. This is particularly difficult to treat in a foreign country because of the language problem and the fear of strange surroundings. Usually the reaction to a normal life after years in a camp is more than a sensitive soul can bear. Funds from World Refugee Year have made it possible to provide more institutions and medical centres.

The United Kingdom World Refugee Year Committee set a target of £2,000,000, and finished with £7,302,941 in cash and £1,816,408 in kind (clothing, houses, etc.), making a total of £9,119,349.

While the money collected in the United Kingdom went mainly to help the refugees in Europe, Hong Kong, Arabs in the Middle East, and Algerians in Tunisia and Morocco, other groups in Asia and Africa received help from some voluntary agencies.

THERE ARE STILL REFUGEES

The Secretary General of the United Nations summed up the significance of World Refugee Year in these words:

'This is, in every respect, to be regarded as a beginning, not an end. The refugee problem will be with us, I am afraid, for ever, unless the world turns more peaceful. For that reason it is good if we can solve the problems which have been with us too long and have got rather stale with all the sum of human suffering they have involved. But we should not believe that this is the end of the road. We must anticipate continued needs, and for that reason we must also count on continued assistance.'

World Refugee Year (WRY) ended on 31st May. The United Kingdom Committee held a rally in the Albert

Hall on the 30th May and Inter-Church Aid (now Christian Aid) declared a total of £1,253,500. This was fifty per cent higher than any other voluntary organisation in the British Isles. The High Commissioner for Refugees told us that it was the highest amount raised by any single voluntary organisation in the world taking part in World Refugee Year.

In countless places up and down the country the Churches unitedly took the lead in providing and stimulating efforts for World Refugee Year. This was the first time Christian Aid had raised more than a million pounds and it was reflected in the increased number of refugees to be helped. Large contributions were made to Hong Kong, and the technical training scheme for over five hundred boys is still flourishing under the aegis of the Y.M.C.A. and the Churches. A considerable number of rehabilitation programmes were started among the Arab refugees with Christian Aid 'WRY' funds.

World Refugee Year provided this fresh impetus and much is owed to those young politicians for their suggestion.

Mr. Harold Rogers of the B.B.C. asked me to do a programme on the radio in May 1966 called 'Days of Decision' about need not creed. I was able to use, from the archives, the voices of some of the people who have helped me to make decisions in the last twenty years. I asked that the late Dr. George Bell, Bishop of Chichester, should be one of them. The following extract was used from a New Year's Eve Sermon he had preached on the B.B.C. in 1957.

Dr. George Bell

I hope that this year our Western statesmen will say to the communists, 'We admire the genius which produced the sputniks, though we don't like the way you treat your satellite states. Let's pull down the screen of hatred and suspicion that divides us.'

With stocks of hydrogen bombs and atom bombs piling up in non-stop competition on both sides, we're all walking on a razor's edge. Sooner or later we have got to live together if we are to survive—it is either co-existence or co-extinction. We must tackle our various disarmament and political problems now, one by one. If necessary let us call in an umpire, independent of both blocks, to preside over our talks and keep us at it till we do agree, in the name of justice, peace and good of the human race. So as we pass into 1958 with the striking of Big Ben, I ask you to take these two ideas with you. First, get the right focus for your life—that is put Christianity into the middle of your building. Next, don't have any more iron screens but take the Christian teaching about loving all your fellow human beings seriously and apply it everywhere.

Dr. Bell worked for refugees for years and was responsible for a large immigrant programme for the Jewish refugees who came to this country between 1932 and 1939. A few days after the broadcast I received a letter from a woman listener which described her experience in an internment camp and just what it meant to be lonely and unhappy in a strange land and to have someone going the extra mile to understanding. The important action was not the preaching of a sermon but a practical expression of Christianity, which is what Christian Aid is all about.

After I had listened to your broadcast talk last Friday, I thought that a small contribution to the memory of Dr. George Bell, Bishop of Chichester, might be of some interest to you.

I have to go far back to the year 1940. I was among the many women who were interned in the Isle of Man. Most of us were Jewish 'Refugees from Nazi Oppression' and, at the same time, (paradoxically) 'Enemy Aliens' in this country.

It is difficult after such a long lapse of time to describe the mental atmosphere in the Internment Camp. We were far from the war as such and yet deeply involved in its happenings.

As 'Internees' we had no access to newspapers, letters arrived sparingly and with long delay and, of course, censored. It was an exceptionally beautiful summer, but the blue sky, the sea, the dunes and hills of the island could not succeed in allaying the unrest and worries of the women who were separated from their families and friends. Rumours spread like wildfire and filled the atmosphere to choking point. Somehow the news reached us about the disaster of the *Andorra Star*—mothers and wives were filled with anxiety.

The Commandant and her Assistants, without malice, had no idea whom they had to supervise and take charge of—a 'rather mixed lot' they said and, in some respect, they were right. Besides some country girls mainly from Austria, the majority were Jewish women from Germany and Austria, Christian wives of 'non-Aryan' clergymen, politicians and journalists who had opposed the Nazi régime.

We seemed to be forgotten. A young Methodist priest opened his church for all who had the desire to participate in the Sunday service and worship—and there were many: 'Need not Creed'.

One day, in June or July 1940 (if I remember rightly), a notice appeared on the church door that the

Bishop of Chichester would preach and conduct next Sunday's service.

The church was crowded and Dr. Bell found the words which reached our hearts. His message was that we 'Refugees' too had a mission: 'to be ambassadors of goodwill'.

After the service, a wave of deeply moved women surged up to the altar where the Bishop stood in his ecclesiastical attire. He was obviously strongly impressed, but he felt that he could not cope with the many questions and grievances put to him by the excited crowd. He suggested a meeting that same evening in the church hall and to prepare a list of our main problems. And he came, now in civilian clothes, and listened. He listened with patience and understanding. Thus he became for us, on our island, a bridge (physically and spiritually) to the world at large, to reality and humanity.

What he achieved in practical terms, we never knew; he himself was never allowed to come again to the camp, but his human approach and kindness was the greatest possible comfort for all present, and an unforgettable experience.

I felt after your talk that I owe this expression of gratitude to the memory of Dr. George Bell, Bishop of Chichester.

ARAB REFUGEES

In 1954 I wrote a report of my first visit to the Middle East. I had been greatly disturbed and unhappy but at the same time moved by my experience, and it still holds good today.

My first visit to the Bible lands was in 1954. I arrived

in Beirut and had a morning in which to 'wallow' in the first enjoyable reactions produced by the transition in a few hours from the New World to the Old. My hotel bedroom was on the first floor and literally overhanging the beautiful Beirut bay with its bright blue sea and the snow-capped Lebanese hills rising up from the town. I watched two Arab fishermen for hours, seemingly motionless and apparently not catching any fish. They were there each day from dawn to sunset looking exactly like a picture in the Bible I used to see when a child. I never really believed in those pictures until Christmas, 1954.

Two days later I visited a number of Arab refugee camps and came down to earth with a bump. I shall not easily forget three women sitting on their haunches with tin bowls in their hands waiting for the food centre to open. They were dressed in the usual Arab women's fashion of a drab black, long coat-like garment over an assortment of cast-off American clothes, with faces and heads half covered. Their eyes were dumb-like and their patience was of eternity. They were as stone and looked as though they had been waiting with those bowls from the beginning of time. All round that particular camp is the most beautiful scenery, colourful and not so desolate as other mountainous areas in that part of the world. This mound of humanity was like an open wound, swollen and running with filthy matter, on a beautiful body. The patient fatalism of the Muslim in his belief in God and that in time God will cease his punishment and will then restore him to his former state, is difficult for Western Christians to understand. While we might cry, 'How long, O Lord, how long?' we would continue to protest politically or try to put it right in some way or other; even if disappointment was inevitable, we would keep on trying to be 'practical'.

There are many refugee camps all over the Middle

East. As well as refugees officially recognised by the United Nations and living in camps and in slums in the towns, there are the inhabitants of the villages bordering on Israel who are known as economic refugees; they have not lost their homes and status but have lost their livelihood, owing to the geographical position of their villages. Because of lack of funds, these unhappy communities do not come within the scope of the United Nations for food and other amenities as do the Palestinian refugees, and they are almost destitute. Some houses and smallholdings are half in Israel and half in Jordan and many small olive groves are divided by the imaginary armistice line. In Britain, in a comparable situation in a suburb, it would be a matter of life and death for a householder to go down to his compost heap at the bottom of the garden. There it is more serious because his olive trees are his only means of earning a living.

A NEW STATE IS BORN

In 1948 the United Nations, under great pressure from the United States and the United Kingdom, declared Palestine to be the new state of Israel. The Palestinian Arabs living there and the Arabs in the surrounding countries were united in their opposition to this decision. The tragedy is that the roots of both Jews and Arabs are deeply embedded in the Middle East and they are closely related in culture.

As a result of the declaration, a war between Israel and the neighbouring Arab countries broke out within a short time of the creation of the new State. Something like 886,000 Arabs became refugees. It was an all-too-familiar episode. When countries are arbitrarily partitioned by foreign powers or victorious armies, then a refugee population is created and the seeds of long-term hatred sown.

Undoubtedly some well-to-do Arab families left earlier and established themselves in Egypt, the Lebanon and other places. The Israeli Government claims that the Arabs were urged to stay in their homes but were persuaded by their leaders to leave, being assured that they would be able to return in a few days. Refugee leaders deny this and affirm they were forced to leave. Whatever the differing circumstances surrounding political and wartime refugees, such confused statements always prevail. It is well-nigh impossible to get at the truth. What we do know is that the inevitable happened and hundreds of thousands of ordinary and mostly simple people were exiled from their homes to wait outside their own border until a political settlement was secured and they could return home. They are still waiting. For many years prior to the Second World War there had been Jews living in Palestine, but by 1947 thousands more had arrived as refugees escaping from Hitler's persecution or on release from concentration camps. It was then that a large proportion—but not all—of the world Jewry demanded even more strongly than before 1949 that they should return from exile to what they claimed was historically their rightful national home. This pressure was primarily concentrated in the United States, and as a result the United Nations agreed to the partition of Palestine. The war was fought with bitterness on both sides and it would seem that the hatred engendered by the war has increased rather than decreased.

One of the terrible results of war is what it does to men when they are fighting each other, and often things happen which their leaders did not foresee or desire. Rules and orders in border wars and riots are forgotten in the heat of the battle. On 9th April 1948 an Arab village called Deir Yasin was attacked and all the civilians in sight, including women and children, were killed. Two hundred dead bodies were found by United Nations investigators. Thousands of Arabs fled from their homes in Israel, never to return. Many Jewish leaders were horrified at what had happened, but there was no going back. The full circle had turned, Hitler was the last straw for the Jews in Germany and they were fighting to make a national home for themselves, and so Arabs in turn became refugees. Since then Arabs have brutally killed Israelis, and so it goes on—an all-too-familiar human tragedy.

THE UNITED NATIONS

The United Nations set up an organisation to care for the refugees called the United Nations Relief and Works Agency for Palestine Refugees in the Near East known as U.N.R.W.A. At the end of the war in 1949 ration cards were provided for every refugee. These cards enable a refugee to get bare subsistence, but no ration cards have been issued for new-born babies since that time. As it is estimated that 25,000 babies are born each year, it is obvious that a large number of people have to live on very little food. In addition, U.N.R.W.A. provides housing, medical care, education and other welfare facilities, but with all this help it only works out at about £10 per refugee per year. Half of the refugees are in Jordan, and the remainder are spread out between Gaza, the Lebanon and Syria. During the years since U.N.R.W.A. started, practically all tented camps have been eliminated and stone 'prefab' housing settlements have replaced them.

VOLUNTARY AGENCIES

It is quite obvious that U.N.R.W.A. does not have sufficient money to meet the needs, and so the Churches and voluntary agencies carry out a large supplementary programme. The largest agencies are the Christian Churches and they work mainly in two groups, although there is close co-operation. They are the Pontifical Mission, which is Roman Catholic, working directly from the Vatican, and the Near East Christian Council Refugee Committee, which administers Christian aid sent from churches all over the world. The Near East Christian Council Refugee Committee is representative of the Arab Christian Churches, the Lutheran World Federation, the foreign missionary societies, the Y.M.C.A. and the Y.W.C.A. They regularly distribute food and clothing, mostly from America, and also provide supplementary education, medical care and housing, self-help programmes and vocational training. Practically all the aid for the border villages is carried out by the Christian agencies, and they co-operate with the Muslim relief groups.

Every year at the General Assembly of the United Nations a report is given of the work of U.N.R.W.A. and an impassioned appeal made for a larger budget. Unfortunately, the budget is never met and there were doubts at one time as to whether U.N.R.W.A. would be able to continue after 1960, when its allotted term came to an end, but the mandate has been regularly renewed. Most of the money given to the U.N.R.W.A. comes from the United States and the United Kingdom. During this time until June 1967 many people—both official and otherwise—tried to bring Arabs and Jews together to discuss reconciliation, but without success. Israel claims

to have always acknowledged her share of the responsibility for the Arab refugees. The refugees, however,
would not consider resettlement under any terms except
to return to their own country. At a distance, you may
feel critical and say that after twenty years this is unreal,
that they will never get back to their own homes and besides Israel is established in a most remarkable way.
Jewish refugees are still arriving in Israel from Rumania
and North Africa, and they are struggling to establish
once and for all a rightful national security. But imagine
what you would do if you were arbitrarily banished to
another county or country. Wouldn't you insist that the
only place you would go would be back home?

FIVE-DAY WAR IN 1967

The Daily Express published in July 1967 a 'Photo-
news Colour Special' with the title 'The Five-Day War
and After'. The first photograph across two pages
showed the desert with four dead Arabs and across the
top were the words 'There was no water, no food, four
died near a desert road that led to nowhere.' The well-
known foreign correspondent, James Cameron, described
vividly the start of the third war in the Middle East since
1948. It lasted five days. He wrote:

> The short hot summer of 1967 saw history jolted off
> course with a violence so abrupt and stunning that the
> explosion was over almost before the shock waves
> broke.
> There are many sad and angry arguments, for
> which this is not the place. But from Beirut to the
> Atlas Mountains lay a huge dark lake of hatred. Twice
> before it had overflowed; 1948 and in 1956. In June

the dam burst again.

On the morning of Monday, June 5, as I was about to load my bag on the London plane, the air-raid sirens of Tel Aviv began to sound; Kol Israel radio broke the air with the news that the balloon had at last gone up. The attack had begun.

I have, unfortunately, seen quite a few battle-fields, but never anything like this. It was an armoured engagement much greater in volume and in scope than El Alamein (which none of us had realised at the time). On this dreadful homeless wilderness some tens of thousands of Egyptians had been killed or captured or—the poignant thing that tormented the imagination —fled to wander in pockets and clutches aimlessly through the burning, waterless heat.

Jerusalem suffered. The exultation of a Jewish conquest of the Old City and the Wailing Wall after two millenia could not conceal the big price that had been paid.

The overwhelming of the west bank of the Jordan has, for the time being, straightened a frontier, and with it imposed military and administrative problems, with a million more refugees, that would stretch the capabilities of a Moses.

The lightning hammer-blow is over, but the end, most assuredly, is not yet.

HELP FROM THE CHURCHES

The World Council of Churches sent staff members at the very outset of the war to work out with the Churches, the refugee committee there and with U.N.R.W.A. how best to help to organise the 'aftermath' of the war devastation and the large number of 'new' refugees. The 'new' is ironical because they were old refugees from 1949 and now new but a few miles away from where they were before. An appeal was issued from the World Council for two million U.S. dollars. Christian Aid sent over £100,000, Germany £200,000 and the United States provided one million U.S. dollars. The Lutheran World Federation and the Roman Catholics made simultaneous appeals and received a good response.

A new emergency committee was set up in Jerusalem, made up of all the Church agencies and voluntary bodies under the chairmanship of the Anglican Archbishop. Among them they provided large quantities of food and clothing, and medicaments were distributed. Plans are in hand for overall relief and rehabilitation, including rebuilding the severely damaged frontier villages. The newly displaced persons included 200,000 to be looked after in East Jordan, 35,000 in the United Arab Republic West of the Suez Canal from Sinai and another 200,000 from the Gaza Strip and Southern Syria, a large number of them already registered with U.N.R.W.A.

From the outset, thousands of Arab families moved from the immediate area of conflict, to be joined in the days and weeks that followed by many thousands more from territories newly occupied by the armed forces of Israel. For these people, many of whom were refugees for the second time in a generation, shelter, food, water and medicine had to be found at once. Essential services also had to be maintained for those Palestine refugees—more than one million in number—who remained in their camps and villages in Lebanon, Jordan, the Syrian Arab Republic and the Gaza Strip.

During the first grim days, new refugees often had no more than a round of Arab bread each day for food and many spent nights in the open, mothers huddling their babies to them in the chill winds on the Jordan heights.

Schools, mosques and other public buildings were quickly thrown open and families crowded in, sometimes forty people to a room. Despite all health precautions, the threat of an epidemic was never far away under such overcrowded conditions, and tented camps were established as soon as the tents arrived, mostly by airlift.

By the spring of 1968, thanks to the generous support of the international community, the hungry had been fed, the sick had been treated; all families had been given some kind of shelter and most children were back in school. But, if the first emergency phase appears to be over, conditions are very far from satisfactory and the future is dark and uncertain. In spite of the chaos and the fears of the people, institutions such as the Y.M.C.A. and the Y.W.C.A. have been patched up and are open again, although the numbers in the trade schools in Jericho are considerably reduced because so many are in camps in Amman. All the organisations have co-operated in a new type of loan programme and long-term projects are in the planning stage. There are frequent sorties on the border and all expect the fighting to break out again in the near future. Perhaps the most important work is the personal service to the individual families.

U.N.R.W.A. REPORTS

U.N.R.W.A.'s statistics have always dealt in 'hundreds of thousands'—the many Arab refugees who have on two occasions fled from their homes in such large numbers. In this context it is not always easy for others to appreciate the individual suffering and strain through which the refugees have to pass—families divided, homes abandoned and hunger a lurking fear. The story of one young refugee should help to promote the necessary understanding. Her name is Khadra Al-Mun'im, a farm labourer's wife and a refugee for the second time in her life. As a little girl in 1948, Khadra fled the village of Beit-Tar, Jerusalem district, with her parents; most of the other villagers left at the same time. After arriving in the Arab-held part of Palestine that became Jordan's West Bank, Khadra's family settled in U.N.R.W.A.'s Dheisheh Camp, in the Hebron district. Over the next nineteen years Khadra went to school, grew up and married. By the time the 1967 conflict began, she and her husband had three children, and were living quietly in the camp. Her husband had work in the summer, so there was a little money to supplement U.N.R.W.A.'s monthly rations. Then, in the confusing situation that followed the outbreak of the hostilities they, like thousands of similar families, had to make an agonising decision—to stay or go?

They went. Walking the mountain-tops at night, avoiding the roads, they took nearly six days getting to the Jordan Valley. Khadra carried Afaf, the baby, just twelve months old, while her husband took the other two children on his back. And as the days went by, all the family reached the state of exhaustion, for they were short of both food and water, but under the burning sun of the Jordanian summer the baby suffered most.

When the family finally crossed the Jordan over the twisted spars of the Allenby Bridge, the infant's skin was already beginning to wrinkle. He should have weighed $8\frac{1}{2}$ kilos ($18\frac{1}{2}$ lb.); in fact he weighed $4\frac{1}{2}$ kilos (10 lb.)—just over ordinary birth weight.

There they were in East Jordan—a family like many thousands of others, with no food, no possessions and nowhere to go. At this point, U.N.R.W.A. was able to help. The family were allocated a tent (at Karemeh extension camp) and provided with blankets and food.

Most important of all, Karemeh Camp has a rehydration/nutrition centre for the treatment of dehydrated babies and Afaf was given the treatment he so urgently needed. Daily solutions of glucose and salts were fed to him under medical supervision; special baby foods were given to his mother to build up his strength. The gastro-enteritis that was debilitating him was being conquered when U.N.R.W.A. first photographed him. That was early in August 1967. When the possibility of returning to the West Bank came up, the family put in an application, but it was not among the small fraction of applications approved. In November, Khadra, her husband and the children were still living in the same tent, facing the storms and floods of winter in the Jordan Valley. Afaf was better, but not much. After regular sessions at the clinic during August and September, Khadra stopped attending as she thought the baby was improving in health and the other children needed her attention. Since then some of the signs of dehydration and malnutrition have returned and Afaf is having regular treatment again.

Unhappily then, there is no end to the story. This is only the beginning.

A similar story could be repeated a hundred times and this personal service is high on the priority list.

HOW MANY REFUGEES IN 1970?

It is always difficult to assess the accurate numbers of refugees. In 1968 the United Nations High Commission for Refugees reported that there were approximately sixteen million refugees in the world. They included nine million in Asia, one million in the Middle East and nearly two million in Vietnam. At that time it was estimated that thirty-five of the fifty-seven countries in Africa had refugees from countries other than their own. These figures represent a large number of people who are shocked, frightened, insecure and lonely.

One Saturday in April 1968 I heard a folk singer on the radio playing his guitar and singing a song by Tom Paxton called 'I can't help but wonder where I'm bound'. Every refugee, every displaced person and every immigrant in Great Britain or elsewhere must moan these words over and over again when at times they feel unwanted and frustrated:

> *'It's a long and dusty road,*
> *It's a hot and heavy load*
> *And the folks I meet ain't always kind.*
> *Some are bad and some are good,*
> *Some have done the best they could,*
> *Some have tried to ease my troblin mind.*
> *And I can't help but wonder where I'm bound,*
> *Where I'm bound,*
> *And I can't help but wonder where I'm bound.'*

3

WORLD HUNGER AND DEVELOPMENT

WORLD HUNGER AND DEVELOPMENT

THE Freedom from Hunger Campaign was launched in 1961 by Dr. B. R. Sen, then the Director of the United Nations Food and Agricultural Organisation. It was planned to last for five years, and education in every country in the world was regarded as important as fund-raising. National committees were set up in most countries in Asia, Africa and Latin America as well as in the West. Subsequently the Campaign was extended for a further five years, becoming the United Nations Development Decade, and included most of the specialised agencies such as the World Health Organisation. The United Kingdom Committee, of which Christian Aid was a founder-member, is still functioning, although the Development Decade has not been an outstanding success. Nations lost interest and did not know how to handle such a long-term diffused programme. Local political upheavals and civil wars in some developing countries hindered progress. Nevertheless, the passionate interest in development remains in many parts of the world. Christian Aid also continues to collaborate with the Food and Agriculture Organisation in Rome over the planning and financing of projects.

The total number of projects financed from Christian Aid's contribution to the Freedom from Hunger Campaign was over 90, costing over two million pounds. They were in 45 countries of Africa, Asia, Latin America, the Caribbean, the Middle East and parts of Europe. The majority but not all by any means were schemes initiated by churches, missions, Councils of

Churches and other ecumenical bodies. It is not possible to describe more than a few of these 'hunger—self-help' projects in which Christian Aid was involved, but they are typical of a world-wide effort. I visited most of the areas and some on several occasions to discuss further plans and to assess priorities.

DEVELOPMENT PROJECTS

Algeria

One of the bloodiest episodes of the post-colonial era was in Algeria, a former French colony. When the war was over the devastation was widespread. Millions of people in Algeria itself had been moved about as the war developed and were living in desperate conditions in inferior encampments. Large numbers were in Morocco and Tunisia and returned to Algeria. The new Government asked the World Council of Churches, the International Red Cross and the Roman Catholic agencies if they would undertake the immediate and urgent relief for the bitter cold winter months following the cease-fire. They agreed and each took roughly a third of the country. I, along with colleagues from related church ecumenical agencies, including the World's Y.M.C.A. and Y.W.C.A. and the Lutheran World Federation, was summoned to Geneva to plan together an emergency programme. We needed two and a half million blankets to allow at least one blanket per person and the necessary food to provide emergency rations for over one and a half million displaced people. It was decided to issue a world-wide appeal for the necessary funds. The majority of the blankets were purchased in Great Britain and Christian Aid arranged the despatch. We bartered with each other round the table about the transfer of ship-loads of wheat. American ships already on their way to other countries were diverted to Algeria, and other countries promised to replace the cargoes as soon as possible so that those for whom the wheat was destined would not suffer too long a delay.

Later, when conditions improved, international ecumenical teams in Algeria conceived a large and imaginative programme of attempting to plant seventy million trees. This was a large reafforestation programme to replace the large areas of forest land burned to the ground by flame-throwing tanks. Christian Aid played a considerable part in this project and it became a major effort during the Freedom from Hunger Campaign. By the time the United Christian programme was handed over to the Algerian Government, twenty million trees had already been planted, related agricultural projects developed and hundreds of people fed and occupied in the process. This was no charity 'hand out' because during the period hundreds of workers were paid the rate for the job in food and other essential amenities. Much of this developed into a permanent self-help and training development operation covering sixty-seven acres of land. There are very few Christians in Algeria but the ecumenical teams were welcome and trusted.

East Africa

I have described elsewhere in this book my visit to Kenya in 1961 when, with the Christian Council of Kenya and the Kenya Government, a large five-year development programme was planned in seven areas for which Christian Aid provided half a million pounds during the Hunger Campaign. My first visit to Kenya was in 1954 when I went to help to provide aid and workers for the victims of the Mau Mau revolution. During these seven years the Christian Council of Kenya had gained considerable experience and felt able to tackle major projects. The planning of the Freedom from Hunger Campaign was a considerable undertaking and we provided an agricultural adviser for the Christian Council at their request, the whole being carried through in close collaboration with the Government. The projects included training schemes for farmers, a pilot project of resettlement and training for Masai farmers, heretofore nomadic, and a fishing development scheme. The result of this wide special development scheme meant the start of a new life for many, and the development of farming skills for young boys and girls was gratifying and productive.

There were similar agricultural training schemes started in Tanzania and Uganda, including Y.W.C.A. programmes for women farm workers. In Sarawak, Chile, Rhodesia, Brazil, Nigeria and many other countries projects were supported by Christian Aid in collaboration with British Missionary Societies. A considerable number of agricultural experts were recruited for limited periods and sent all over the world.

India

'You never miss the water until the well runs dry.' The tragedy of India is that the wells are always running dry, and the people do not have the equipment to drill deep enough into the soil to reach the perpetual waterbeds. India is constantly under the threat of famine, and the provision of water is one of the surest defences.

One of the many examples is the project at Jalna and surounding district, an area with 50,000 inhabitants in the state of Maharashtra which was under the supervision of

John McLeod, who was sent out to India by the Church of Scotland Overseas Council. At first Christian Aid provided him with various types of irrigation equipment for small-scale schemes, and then in 1965 sent him one of the most advanced well-drilling rigs on the market—the *Halco Tiger*, costing £62,000.

The Pioneering Tiger was the first of its kind in India. So successful has it proved that other agencies followed suit and sent in Tigers. Christian Aid also sent one to drill wells in the Bangalore district of India. During 1968 a unit was provided for Ajmer in Ragasthan under the auspices of the Church of Scotland, which included a Halco Drilling Rig with support vehicles and auxiliary equipment for the unit. Many local Christian Aid Committees raised enough money to send a Tiger to India, thus this was a considerable enterprise.

It can truly be said that the Tiger revolutionised well-drilling programmes in India and the Government took the Tiger up in a big way. It can drill through the hardest of rocks to considerable depths and water can nearly always be found, even in the driest seasons.

BOOST FOR BOTSWANA'S AGRICULTURE

During the latter phase of the Freedom from Hunger Campaign Christian Aid and Oxfam jointly agreed to finance two-thirds of a large soil-conservation and dam-building programme in Botswana.

Korea

The war in Korea ended in 1953 when nine million refugees from the industrial North crossed the agreed border to the mostly rural South. The Churches, in co-ordination with the South Korean Government and the World Council of Churches Refugee Service carried out tremendous programmes. Church World Service of the United States provided workers and money and helped to create Korean Church World Service. Later development projects were carried out.

The largest land-reclamation scheme ever attempted in Korea exemplifies better than anything one of the main themes underlying the Freedom from Hunger Campaign— that people should be helped to help themselves.

The battle against the incoming tides of the Yellow Sea began in the summer of 1961 when a thousand Korean war refugee families banded together to fight for 3,000 acres. And they did so on their own initiative without any machinery, without government support and without financial backing.

In reclaiming this large area of land in the Dae Duck Myum area they set themselves a formidable target; for the work involved lifting thousands of tons of soil and rock from nearby hills to make 2,500 yards of dykes 90 feet deep, the washing of ocean salt out of the new land, the provision of an irrigation system and the building of houses to live in.

This was not a government scheme with all the resources of a national exchequer and a Ministry of Works behind it. Nor was it a scheme inspired based on promises of money and materials. It grew out of the resolve of a community of refugee families to acquire for themselves the land—and the life—they needed.

UNAIDED START

When they started work in 1961 they had no assurance of outside help. They had no financial backing and no machinery to help them. Their resources were the soil and the rock of the hills, the joint strength of their bodies and the determination to succeed. Christian Aid, along with other World Council of Churches agencies, provided funds and food and advice so that the Christian Council of Korea could in three years complete four dykes, re-claim large areas of land for agriculture and build a re-servoir. In eight years a large number of people were re-settled and growing their own food.

Brazil

So successful was the Gurupi resettlement scheme that the Government of Brazil came to regard it as a key to developing the jungle interior. This was an initiative of the Refugee Committee of the National Confederation of Churches in Brazil to which Christian Aid contributed over £80,000.

Most of the 22,000,000 people in the north-east of Brazil live in a semi-feudal culture and depend for the most part on the production of sugar and cotton. The annual population increase is six hundred thousand. Heavy internal migration to large urban centres in search of a better living has taken place.

Because there is not enough proper accommodation in the cities many have to live in adobe huts with earth floors and palm-leaf roofs, crowded together on the out-skirts. Such squalid conditions are the breeding ground for disease, and malnutrition is rife; especially among the children.

In an attempt to resettle these families on more pro-ductive land of North Brazil, the state Government re-served 3,000 hectares of land at Gurupi, located along the new highway between Belem and Brasilia.

The Gurupi project was a pioneer enterprise attempting to show that improved agricultural methods and the introduction of suitable industries could rapidly improve the standard of living in the region. The project was launched in 1964.

Vast tracts of jungle were cleared and it is now possible to reach all parts of Gurupi by jeep.

Much land has been tilled, seeds and saplings planted, pigs and chickens bought. A recent report said that the blackbean crop was excellent and so were the peanuts. Attempts to grow cotton failed.

Medical care is as always imperative and a prophylactic service was set up. This introduced an educational programme which included practical demonstrations to stamp out many misconceptions, for example, the widespread belief that malaria was caused by eating fruit. Further health education has meant the spraying of homes, boiling of water, keeping chickens out of the homes and building septic tanks.

The project progressed day by day. Now everyone along the highway believes in the region's future, and near-by villages and towns are rapidly expanding. The atmosphere has been described as exciting, similar perhaps to that in the old American West a hundred years ago.

The Gurupi project is now regarded as a supreme example of what can be done when the land is farmed professionally; so much so, in fact, that many villages in the area, despite their early scepticism, are beginning to follow suit.

WORLD POPULATION

So much has been written about the 'Pill' that it seems academic to mention the frightening increase of population all over the world. This is the common problem of men and women everywhere, but with the possible exception of war, also common to all, it is only common in respect to the facts of the case and not to the solution. We live in a world where, in many places, social injustice is the order of the day, where 15,000 people die of hunger each day, where racial discrimination is practised unnoticed on our doorsteps and where political action is disappointing—a world which is too difficult for most of us to comprehend. In the West although we are only 20 per cent of the world's 3,000 million we have 90 per cent of the world's income, 90 per cent of its gold reserves, 95 per cent of its scientific knowledge, 70 per cent of its meat and 80 per cent of its protein. The annual increase in the national income of the West in 1967 was equal to the entire national income for Latin America and twice that of Africa and India. We are also increasingly inter-related in economic development and must share each other's problems of world hunger if our children and grandchildren are to survive. The voluntary organisations and the Churches should press for World Poverty to climb up nearer to the top of the 'top ten'.

A joint conference of representatives from the World Council of Churches and from the Roman Catholic Secretariat for Peace and Justice was held in Beirut in April 1968 on World Co-operation and Development. One of the groups discussing Christian conviction and motivation opened their report, which was unanimously accepted, with—

'Why do we Christians concern ourselves with the development, the full human development, of the world? Quite simply because we believe that it is God's will, and that this concern and the action that follows from it is laid down upon us as human beings by our Creator.'

The major question for us all is how to tackle it. Have

we power to 'remove the social and political obstructions to dynamic progress, to see that trade on fair terms is developed between the nations and that all governments, separately and jointly, re-examine their priorities'?

The brutal fact is that it is only the minority of our population in the British Isles who think that overseas aid is the most urgent need of our future and that it is a political priority as well as a personal issue.

REVOLUTION

In many countries of the world today students and others are in revolution and many are ready to use violence in order to force society in their countries to change their structures, assuming that this will release their own frustrations and help the developing countries and ensure that the world can achieve social justice and peace. The word revolution is difficult to stomach by Western governments and the British in particular. It is not respectable, it frightens us and we think of it as being more at home in Latin America or Eastern Europe. Revolution doesn't necessarily mean violence but it sometimes does. We should remember that for the same reason the French Revolution, the Russian Revolution, the revolt of the peasants in Germany and the series of bloody civil wars which went on for years in these islands took place. These historical incidents including 'religious' wars irrevocably contributed much to our culture and life as it is today. Whether the Negroes in the United States will get their rights without violence is not an academic question but a real one. How can I, sitting in my comfortable flat and free to go where I wish, condemn those who, sick of the years and years of frustration, resort to violence to get their freedom?

The risks are tremendous and terrifying and no-one, least of all Christians, can avoid facing these questions with the utmost care. One thing is certain: men everywhere are not going to be pushed around and automatically do as they are told, when their proper demands for justice are either ignored or postponed indefinitely. They will find it difficult to avoid violence because non-violence seems to be entirely ineffective. It won't be the first time in history that men have used violence without declaring war in order to get peace and justice. In the heat of emotion caused by injustice the irony of the situation is the use of violence for the securing of peace and justice.

This places a tremendous burden on the Churches. Violence is the antithesis of the Christian faith but the Churches seem loth to change their attitude to society in order to bring hope to men struggling for justice. The stubborn resistance to structural changes in the life and work of the Church in order to meet the needs of today may well ultimately kill the Church as we know it. Its real life is eternal but its 'cosiness' must go.

I am totally sympathetic to the dilemma because I find it hard to keep my integrity and am afraid to lose the security of the 'establishment'. We need to make an effort to get into the political battle; we should persuade ourselves that development is necessary for all men and see that world poverty is the greatest menace of our time. This calls for immediate change at home as well as overseas, and Christian Aid is only one of the ecumenical opportunities to point to the needs of men by giving aid and influencing political decisions. But at the end of the day it is an individual responsibility.

'DO-GOODERS'

It is the fashion of many young people to speak disparagingly about so-called 'do-gooders'. But both at home and abroad a large number of old and young are doing precisely that—'doing good' by helping the homeless in the British Isles as well as abroad, many offering to go overseas to help disaster victims and aid programmes. The expressed abhorrence of the word is a revolt against the past when social action meant providing soup kitchens during the depression in the thirties, and before that the rich delivering soup and food parcels to the cottages of the poor. Few remember those days, but it is all written down in the various social histories of Great Britain. The word 'do-gooder' has persisted. Unfortunately we include in one word the self-righteous, pompous dispenser of crumbs from the rich table to the beggar at the door, Schweitzer, Florence Nightingale, Wilberforce and the middle-class men and women, who at the beginning of this century founded, in the face of great opposition, most of the social service we enjoy in this country today. There were the Tolpuddle Martyrs, the Charity Organisation Society, now the Family Welfare Association, and a whole army of thoughtful industrialists and organisations who pioneered and provided us with the rights we now possess.

This has provided a background for the modern voluntary organisation. The truth is that there have never been as many armies of 'do-gooders' as there are today. The well-known large organisations, including those working for social service in Britain and those for overseas aid, attract support and service from large numbers of individuals. These organizations are to a greater or lesser degree sophisticated and mechanised and might be termed 'big business' or 'Charity Ltd'. They have professional publicity departments and public relations advisers. The transference of funds and goods by the aid bodies is handled efficiently and projects are carefully checked overseas. All are to some extent controlled by the Charity Commissioners. Those who are international in the proper understanding of the word transfer the direction of the projects to the indigenous people in the country concerned. They work closely with the United Nations and governments.

In addition there are thousands of voluntary organisations of all sizes, many quite small with 'repeat' mandates of the larger organisations. Hardly a week passes without a new organisation with the same objects as the others arising, like the phoenix from the ashes, claiming a new insight and special qualifications. This happens all over Europe and North America, and increasingly in Asia, Africa and Latin America.

It is hard enough for the large organisations to retain integrity and avoid paternalism and the old meaning of 'do-gooder'. It is extremely hard for the small new bodies who hope to see, literally, how every penny is spent and to have person-to-person contact with the receivers of aid. Sometimes they wish to add religious or political strings to their giving. While we might well be critical of the muddle-headedness and limited vision of many of the innumerable 'one-man-shows', nevertheless one must be thankful that British citizens have retained the capacity to respond to calls for help. Theirs is a revolt, and maybe a losing one, against the seeming depersonalisation of modern society and even 'professional charity' in a growing technological society and at a time when the beginning of the space age has projected new visions and limitless development.

This is a new version of the excellent sense of responsibility found in the middle classes fifty years ago which we have not quite replaced in the present generation. Somehow we must constantly rethink how best to narrow the gap between mass media, over-simplification in publicity, demonstrations and the like and a broader and deeper sense of British responsibility towards World Poverty.

THE FUNCTIONS OF THE VOLUNTARY ORGANISATIONS

The *raison d'être* of a voluntary organisation, whether working at home or abroad, is to be free to pioneer and to be in the front line when need is apparent. While it should work whenever possible with government and the United Nations, and provide workers, it must also retain its freedom to agitate for the rights of those in need when the State and the community are falling short of their responsibilities. Those organisations and Churches involved in development projects such as agriculture, urban and rural development, refugees and neo-refugees and disasters, clearly we must raise money. It is a prime function that cannot be dodged. It is important that all should be constantly proclaiming that voluntary agencies are pioneering efforts by indigenous people helped by others from all over the world. They can be related to governments and the United Nations agencies but they must be content with an ancillary role. They can help new nations during the intermediary stage, when they have to make agonising decisions about priorities and at the same time are fighting battles to be economically solvent. The human aid to each other at this stage is most important. When the voluntary organisations go out to raise their money they should always bear this in mind, or the importance of education and political action will be overlooked. Every care should be taken to see that the projects are possible and that the donors are not paternalistic in their approach. It is also important that those same people should take part in their own local communities by tackling social injustice and welfare and other related problems at home.

Another important task is not to be discouraged when it is obvious that all the background understanding is beyond the ordinary person, for these people are often from the backbone of an organisation and need understanding. There are people available who do have the knowledge and are articulate and who should be used as catalysts; their help should be sought to provide information on development in the language of the ordinary person.

The people who agitate to unite all the organisations in one enormous take-over bid are mistaken. They each have their own ethos, and their supporters need to get the satisfaction of working through the organisation of their choice. Very often a new and inspired organisation helps the older ones to get a new impetus. Shelter is an important and typical example. Co-operation with each other and understanding of each other's *raison d'être* is essential to prevent overlapping and undignified competition. For example, Save the Children Fund, Oxfam and Christian Aid have common aims but a different ethos, although supporters sometimes serve the three bodies. Oxfam and Save the Children Fund help Churches all over the world, sometimes through missionary societies and all are most grateful. Increasingly they work together, especially in time of disasters, in joint educational programmes and political agitation. But the indigenous Churches in other countries, mostly members of the World Council of Churches, have the right to expect help from the world-wide Christian family and they see their own central body, namely the Division of Inter-Church Aid, Refugee and World Service, as their ecclesiastical United Nations carrying out their own relief and service agency. In the British Isles this means Christian Aid.

INTERNATIONAL CHRISTIAN AID

There is often a mistaken understanding of the role of the World Council of Churches' Division of Inter-Church Aid, as though it were simply a middleman for passing on funds from the wealthy west to the poorer countries. This is far from the truth. The staff and committees involved in this operation in Geneva are representative of all continents. All projects come through the indigenous National Christian Councils to Geneva. When I first went to Kenya in 1954 at the height of the Mau Mau rebellion, the Christian Council of Kenya was all white faced except for two Africans who, at any rate when I attended their meeting, both then and during my following two annual visits, never uttered a word. Now their quite considerable staff are all African except for two or three expatriate specialists, and by far the majority of the committee and all the officers are African. This is typical of all Councils affiliated to the All Africa Conference of Churches which in the main consists of the churches on the continent of Africa who are members of the World Council. At their Assemblies only members may vote, although there may be Western guests present.

The same applies to the East Asian Christian Conference, with a similar constitution, which from the beginning has managed its own affairs and decided on its own priorities. Both bodies received help from churches round the world towards their refugee and aid programmes but not by any means all, because increasingly they are paying their way. Similar co-ordinating councils are developing in Latin America, the Pacific and the Middle East.

In times of emergency when an appeal goes out from Geneva there are small donations from the African, Asian and Latin American Churches. The East Asian Christian Conference has its own team in Vietnam working independently but closely with the larger and wider ecumenical team instigated by the American Churches.

When the National Council of Churches of the United States started the Mississippi Delta Ministry project to help the terrible straits of the Negroes there, and there was hostility and loss of support to the Council, small gifts went to that project through the World Council of Churches from poor Churches in Asia and Africa as well as from Great Britain, Germany and other countries in Europe.

The two hundred and nine member Churches of the World Council have committed themselves to world-wide programmes of aid and development without evangelical strings attached. It is in the realm of development and the search after peace and justice that close collaboration with the Roman Catholic Church is to be found. Most can sink their theological differences when working together for those in need. This is not unity in theological depth but pioneering action which illuminates the truth of the Christian Gospel. It is quite clear that before long the Roman Catholic and World Council meetings to discuss development will begin to widen into planning joint programmes for development. This will not be difficult because already the agencies centred both in Rome and Geneva have planned and carried out projects in collaboration with governments, the United Nations High Commissioner for Refugees and the Food and Agricultural Organisation to mention only three. Four years ago the Muslim Government of Tunisia asked the World Council for six highly trained social workers to start schools for training social workers and to see the first period of training through. The Shah said he knew that the World Council of Churches was Christian but he also knew they would not proselytise. The Council would, he said, produce efficient social workers who had had a proper understanding of what a Christian vocation of service was meant to be as it served man, whatever his political or religious creed. Two of the six were recruited by Christian Aid from these islands.

Christian Aid is the official British section of this ecumenical service and I see it containing a reconciliation content that is wider than a concern about the united work of the Churches. The Church is in society and when it forgets that it is sterile. Christian Aid therefore is anxious that the Churches should work with all organisations who want to tackle world poverty and development, whatever their creed or none. There is obviously a particular function for the Churches in the field of aid and development through which they must bear witness to their calling and their unity but this involves co-operation with all who have a common concern.

A well-known Indian Christian, Professor S. L. Parmar, an economist, speaking at a major ecumenical conference about economic development, urged the Churches to agitate for better terms for trading between the developed and developing nations which, he said, means sacrifice and the changing of established structures, and finished by saying:

But let not structures obscure the importance of the person. When we talk about resources we must recognise two important components: material resources and human resources. To me the latter is of greater significance as it creates and uses material resources. Sometimes we are too obsessed with material resources. Let us develop an obsession for human resources. We must deal with persons, but when we talk of love we are not being sentimental. It is because of our love for our neighbour that we must be interested in his total situation. A person, a person in community, a person influenced by and influencing structures of society. This indeed would be Christian charity—taking men and social processes seriously.

This surely is the proper mandate for all voluntary organisations whatever their ethos. They should all develop an obsession for human resources.

4

DISASTERS AND WAR VICTIMS

INDIA AND PAKISTAN

THE West Pakistan Christian Council sent a telegram on the 8th October, 1965 to the World Council of Churches' Division of Inter-Church Aid:

FOLLOWING RESOLUTION IS FORWARDED BY EXECUTIVE SECRETARY WEST PAKISTAN CHRISTIAN COUNCIL WITH UNANIMOUS APPROVAL CHURCH WORLD SERVICE COMMITTEE FOR IMMEDIATE ASSISTANCE FOR 200,000 PERSONS WITH APPROVAL OF GOVERNMENT OF PAKISTAN STOP PAKISTAN HAVING HONOURED THE CALL OF UNITED NATIONS ORGANISATION SECURITY COUNCIL FOR CEASEFIRE OF HOSTILITIES BETWEEN INDIA AND PAKISTAN THE WEST PAKISTAN CHRISTIAN COUNCIL COMMITTEE OF CHURCH WORLD SERVICE PAKISTAN THANKS GOD FOR HIS ACTION AND RESOLVES THAT AFTER CONSULTATION WITH THE GOVERNMENT OF PAKISTAN MINISTRY OF HEALTH AN APPEAL BE MADE TO THE CHURCHES IN ALL PARTS OF THE WORLD TO SEND HELP FOR WAR SUFFERERS SPECIALLY CIVILIAN REFUGEES FROM OPERATIONAL AREAS STOP IN PURSUANCE WITH THE RESOLUTION OF THE EXECUTIVE COMMITTEE OF THE WORLD COUNCIL OF CHURCHES ON HUMAN NEEDS REQUEST THE INTERCHURCH AID DIVISION TO SECURE THE FOLLOWING AID FOR THE PEOPLE OF PAKISTAN IN THEIR APPEAL FOR WORLD FREEDOM FROM HUNGER CAMPAIGN TO BE LAUNCHED DURING OCTOBER 16 TO 24 1965 STOP 24,000 POUNDS OF FOODGRAINS 20,000 BLANKETS DOLLARS 160,000 FOR 40,000 QUILTS TO BE PURCHASED IN PAKISTAN 200,000 SWEATERS OR COATS FOR MEN WOMEN AND CHILDREN.

This was followed by a letter to the late Dr. Leslie Cooke which included more detail—

The Indian aggression which came in the form of an undeclared war, has caused a considerable damage to the civil population in the border areas and a very large number of people have been uprooted from their homes. It is not possible at present to gauge the exact amount of damage to them, but it would be of considerable magnitude. The Churches in Pakistan are solidly behind the Government authority to do all that they can to help the refugees and the suffering people. I assure you that every possible effort would be made to assist our suffering and displaced Pakistani brethren. An appeal has already been made to the Inter-Church Aid bodies with the permission of the Government of Pakistan, and I am sure the response will be very generous. Any help that can be given will be of great use and assistance and will be very much appreciated. The winter season is setting in fast, and besides foodstuff, warm clothes, quilts and blankets are also urgently needed. I am sure the urgency of the need would be realised and the needed commodities will be despatched as early as possible.

On the 15th October a cable came from the Committee on Relief and Gift Supplies, the relief agency of the Christian Council of India:

REHABILITATION NEEDS NOT YET CLEAR BECAUSE FORWARD AREAS STILL UNSTABLE STOP REQUIRE CLOTHING BEDDING STOP WILL INFORM ADDITIONAL NEEDS NEXT WEEK.

This was followed by a letter to the Rev. Alan Brash,

at that time acting as Asia Secretary at the World Council of Churches headquarters in Geneva:

The following is the summary of the conditions as we find them in the Punjab–Kashmir areas of India at the present time:

1. There is considerable movement of people from the border areas to the interior areas. They have not as yet established permanent camps because these people seem to be on the move. Local communities with the help of district officers are doing a good job of meeting the immediate needs for food and rest of the people in transit.

2. In the area above Amritsar, roughly between Amritsar and Pthankot and Jammu, and north, there are about 100,000 people being evacuated and are in a dozen or more camp centres. Here again the Government has done a first rate job of taking care of these people from the standpoint of food, rest, medical attention, etc.

3. Our staff is prepared to go into the Jammu area as soon as the Government feels it is appropriate to see what help should be given there.

The Commission of the Churches on International Affairs in its report of 1965/66 mentioned the 'deterioration of the situation along the cease-fire line established in 1949 in Kashmir and the occurrence of armed conflict between Pakistan and India in August 1965'. After the United Nations Security Council on 4th September called on India and Pakistan to cease-fire and withdraw to the cease-fire line, cables were sent to the Christian Councils of India, West Pakistan and East Pakistan expressing deep concern and offering support for any action taken to encourage moves to peace.

A message was sent to the same Councils on behalf of the British Council of Churches signed by the Archbishop of Canterbury and Dr. Ernest Payne. The officers of the East Asia Christian Conference, which includes all the member Churches of the World Council of Churches in Asia, also carried on considerable correspondence.

The role of the World Council of Churches and all related service agencies, including Christian Aid in the British Isles, is not to take sides in any war or political emergency but to help all in need. Large sums of money were sent from all the agencies to Geneva, and large quantities of material aid from the United States, Germany and other countries was shifted immediately. Long after the fighting ceased considerable help was given to repair houses, build new ones, provide wells and start up rehabilitation programmes.

In 1964 there was an influx of refugees from East Pakistan into India which was basically a religious disturbance. The programme of rehabilitation was almost wholly carried out by the National Christian Council of India's refugee committee in collaboration with the government. These refugees had to be permanently resettled.

During the past year the Relief Committee has provided the refugees with agricultural machinery, farming implements, animals, seeds, building materials and medical supplies, together with all the technical assistance necessary, totalling a cost of well over half a million rupees. Thirty thousand acres in the east Indian states of Assam, Uttar Pradesh and Madhya Pradesh have been granted to the refugees.

The refugees in Assam were given seven hundred food-producing acres, and reclaimed another eight hundred acres.

In Uttar Pradesh three hundred acres of land in the

district of Hastinapur, allotted to seventy refugee families, have been reclaimed. Of these seventy families ten know nothing of farming, for they have lived from fishing all their lives. To provide them with a living the Committee on Relief and Gift Supplies stocked a local river with ten thousand young fish. To make these Hastinapur communities as self-supporting as possible, the Committee have provided a primary school, dispensary and a community hall. The area has been planted with mango trees and many settlers have been encouraged to develop kitchen-gardens in their backyards. The refugee women are being taught to contribute to community life. Two needlework teachers gave classes in all stages of sewing to women in both Hastinapur and in the Mana district of Madhysa Pradesh. Some 160 women have been trained and are now working in a garment factory created by the government.

This type of programme was carried out in all the areas where the refugees were to be found. Christian Aid sent considerable contributions and some of the expatriates helping were recruited in this country.

There is not room to describe in detail the numerous war emergencies of this kind that have received 'ecumenical' help.

VIETNAM

From the very beginning of the war in Vietnam the usual process of telegrams, emergency meetings all round the world, the relief and other aid from the Churches co-ordinated by the World Council of Churches started immediately. The East Asia Christian Conference representing the main stream of the churches in Asia decided to organise a team to be called Asian Christian Service. Their personnel and the funds were all initially found by the Asian Churches themselves, but as things became worse we all had to help. As I write there are fifteen Asian team members doing social work among the refugees, organising schools and various types of general social work. They live very primitively, suffer from the frequent Viet-Cong attacks and, more particularly, they are harassed in a terrifying way in the Tet offensive.

The American Churches through Church World Service have a considerable programme called the Vietnam Christian Service, with a large international staff working as teams in various parts of Vietnam. The two services work together in close collaboration; large quantities of material goods are distributed, hospitals are manned and every kind of social programme is organised when conditions allow. They are helping the two million refugees, the thousands in hospital burnt with napalm bombs, and look after the children whose parents have been killed and are wandering about lost and frightened.

Christian Aid, along with other agencies related to the World Council of Churches, contributed in a three-month period a total of £250,000. This was in addition to considerable U.S. dollars raised by the American Churches, who also recruited many relief workers and medical personnel. Through the Red Cross, contributions have gone to North Vietnam for medical supplies, a field hospital and surgical kits. Christian Aid has received £70,000 through a special appeal for Vietnam in the last six months and recruited a social worker.

'ACTS OF GOD'

Christian Aid collaborates with sister agencies through the World Council of Churches wherever there is a disaster such as an earthquake, floods, civil war, but especially in emergencies described in legal language as acts of God. Recent disasters supported with money and personnel including earthquakes in Skopje in Yugoslavia and Turkey. Rebuilding of housing areas and villages were particular contributions which the governments asked the World Council of Churches to provide. I had the honour, as vice-Chairman of the World Council of Churches' Division of Inter-Church Aid, Refugee and World Service, to receive a plaque for the World Council of Churches from the Yugoslavian Ambassador to Switzerland who at that time was a woman. Earlier we were involved in the relief of the Agadir and Iran disasters.

There is in Britain a Disasters Emergency Committee comprising the Red Cross, Oxfam, Save the Children Fund, War on Want and Christian Aid. It meets under the auspices of the Red Cross and is called together when there is an 'act of God' disaster large enough to ask for a special television or radio appeal. Sudden emergencies, such as the Middle East War in 1967 and more recently an escalation of the war in Vietnam, are regarded as being appropriate for a joint appeal. The five organisations take turns in handling the administration and the funds are allocated according to the various programmes of the organisations. This has been of great value to Christian Aid when money is needed suddenly; our contribution can then be made more quickly and overlapping is avoided.

There is not space to describe the twenty or more sudden emergencies that involve Christian Aid every year. Some are small but many are large, such as the earthquake in Turkey, when many people were made homeless. We were able to contribute a sizeable sum of money from the Disasters Emergency Fund, and with money which poured into the World Council two villages were rebuilt. The victims of war in the Middle East, described elsewhere, started as a major emergency. Mau Mau in Kenya was Christian Aid's first revolution emergency of any size; it has now developed into a long-term development programme. Within hours of seeing something on television or hearing it on the news the telephone is calling Christian Aid from Geneva. Mr. B. J. Dudbridge, Deputy Director of Christian Aid, may be called to the Red Cross and immediately money is transmitted and tents or whatever else is required are being purchased.

SUCCESS OR FAILURE?

Not all projects, disastrous or otherwise, are one hundred per cent successful. The Iran earthquake was a major catastrophe in 1962. Over eleven thousand people were killed and three hundred and fifty-two villages over a wide area were almost entirely destroyed. There is a small Christian Council in Iran, which is overwhelmingly Muslim. As a result of discussions by the officers of the Council and Government officials, it was decided that the World Council of Churches would rebuild a village. An Iranian engineer was found and discussions took place with the local people. They decided to rebuild a village of three hundred houses, alongside the ruins, which would rehouse all the villagers. They were to be single houses, earthquake proof, and in addition a school for girls as well as boys—an innovation—piped water, also new, and a village centre. The Christian Church of Iran is made up mainly of Presbyterians and Anglicans, the total membership being only approximately 3,000. The American Orthodox Church has a membership of 150,000 and their leaders asked for liaison between all concerned and accepted the responsibility for planning and supervision. A Muslim organisation agreed to be responsible for putting up a new mosque.

Just as the project was getting under way an unfortunate tragedy occurred. Christian Aid, as usual, had been involved in the planning in Geneva and our public relations officer, Hugh Samson, and Maurice Rickards our photographer went out to Iran to see what was going on. The engineer drove them round in a jeep which overturned and he was killed. The others were hurt and shocked but escaped with bruises.

This meant looking for another engineer, which held up the plans. Eventually the village was built and many letters of appreciation from the people received. But the villagers were reluctant to live in the houses. The late Geoffrey Murray, the W.C.C. Press Officer of Inter-Church Aid at the World Council of Churches in Geneva, visited the village a year later to evaluate the project. He wrote:

In Spring 1963 Christopher King and I visited the project to see what progress had been made and found those same first 50 houses 'near completion' but entirely unoccupied. The rest of the buildings were in various stages of completion. But a well had been dug and was supplying water, the schools were in session in two of the houses and a weekly clinic was being held in a third.

Objection was taken because the houses, as planned, did not have walled courtyards, according to the Muslim practice, to shelter the women from prying eyes and also to provide space for donkeys, poultry, and other domestic animals. These walls were eventually provided, and in October 1963 the new village called Esmatabad was dedicated. There was a gathering of some 1,600 villagers, a sheep was roasted for the feast, and the keys of all the houses were solemnly handed over to the heads of the families. We were assured in Geneva that all the houses would be occupied the following week.

Nevertheless, difficulties continued to arise. The promised mosque was never built, partly perhaps because the leaders of the responsible body had landed in gaol for political reasons. Despite this, a visiting preacher had warned the villagers to have nothing to do with houses built by a Christian organisation. As late as December 13th 1964, it was reported to the Christian Council of Iran in Teheran that by actual count, the number of houses occupied at Esmatabad was only 154—about one-half the total number. Nevertheless, the Christian Council went ahead and formally handed over the village to the Iranian authorities. Steps were taken to begin closing the account. Later the World Council of Churches was informed in Geneva that relations with the Esmatabad people were extremely tense, so much so that the building committee feared for their personal safety if they were to enter the village. Since December last, nothing more had been reported to Geneva about the number of houses occupied. I was therefore asked to stop over in Iran on my way back from Asia and see what the actual situation was.

On the afternoon of Wednesday October 26th 1965, I drove into Esmatabad with two members of the C.C.I.'s earthquake committee who were now willing to risk being attacked. In fact our reception was friendly. My first thought on seeing street after street of beautifully built brick houses and public buildings with a tall water tower shining like silver in the background, was one of pleasure and surprise that the

Churches could have carried through so large and splendid an enterprise. Three hundred houses cover quite a tidy area and in the mass, particularly when they are as well built as those of Esmatabad, they make a most impressive sight.

But this first thought was at once followed by one of dismay and shock that all these beautiful buildings should be standing in a sea of unrelieved mud. There was not a blade of grass in sight, not a tree, not a single foot of paved path. Before I left I did discover at the farthermost corner of the village some half a dozen pathetic little leafless saplings but nowhere else was there anything to suggest living green.

I visited a number of houses. Some were fully occupied and there were domestic animals in the courtyards. Some houses were being used as barns. Others were entirely empty but the only outward sign of property deterioration was that of broken windows. I asked how many houses were currently occupied and was told 'about one hundred' that is to say, one-third. My own guess is that this was an underestimate. I was told that from time to time some families go off to relatives in Teheran for temporary work, particularly now, when the harvest is gathered and there is no day labour to be obtained locally by the landless. The fact is that *all* the houses are *owned*. I thought it significant that houses are needed for four teachers in the schools but they cannot be accommodated in those that are at present unoccupied. No-one will release them.

In view of all this, are we to describe Esmatabad as a success or a failure?

But before we form a judgement, the project must be set in the context of all that was attempted through the Iran Earthquake Appeal. Esmatabad was only a part of what was done as a consequence of that

$750,000 fund.

In evaluating what has been accomplished at Esmatabad, it should be said that many other agencies have run into the same situation of not having their houses occupied after completion. This includes the Red Lion and Sun, Rotary, the oil companies and others. On my way from Dusadj I stopped to see one new village of forty houses built by a Muslim merchant for earthquake victims. It is a ghost village. Only two houses are occupied. It, too, had been built according to Teheran ideas without courtyard walls and was a long way from the water supply.

Mistakes were made at Esmatabad, but I do not think that anyone in the Christian Council of Iran or the World Council needs to stand in a white sheet because of them. The best advice available was taken and the project was carried out in accordance with Government wishes. It is conceded that Esmatabad is as good as any of the earthquake rebuilding projects. Unfortunately, the advice was not good enough. It might have been appropriate for an urban population, as witness the success of Archbishop Manoukian's project in Teheran, but it was not near enough to conditions in a rural Iranian community. All that we dreamed of in 1962 has not come true, but it has not all been a delusion and waste. At least one hundred houses are occupied and all are owned. They may be occupied one day if the local authorities, who now control the village, ever see fit to raze the old village with a bulldozer.

Nevertheless something has been accomplished. It is surely not over-optimistic to expect that the children now in school will not be content with the old way of life. That is one door Esmatabad has opened. Another is the example of the families already installed. Will not others presently be inspired to follow their example? And a third could be that those villagers who have already become better farmers, because Esmatabad has helped them along, will become models for the rest. Ought we not in faith to regard these things as mustard seeds that may soon burgeon? Certainly I believe that in carrying out the project patiently and persistently in face of every setback, the Churches set an example of Christian compassion and Christian trust. And from first to last, so far as I can tell, they have acted with the liveliest sense of their responsibilities as stewards of donated money.

Finally, Esmatabad has taught us many lessons from which we in the Churches may and should profit. I am reminded of a tiny poem by Piet Heim the Dane. He says, 'The way to wisdom is simple. It can be stated thus: It is to err, and err, and err, less and less and less.'

If Esmatabad helps us to err less it will have accomplished much for the future.

It would be foolish to think that every enterprise will be an absolute success. Physical conditions, the fear of the unknown, ignorance and limited social services are obstacles that take a long time to overcome. The people in those villages will surely learn from the experience and as development programmes progress they are certain to make a contribution of their own.

EMERGENCY IN AFRICA

The World Council of Churches Inter-Church Aid Division and the Inter-Church Aid Department of the British Council of Churches were, until the second

Assembly of the World Council of Churches at Evanston, U.S.A., in 1954, primarily concerned with European refugees and other aid programmes in Europe. The exception was the Middle East and from 1951 large relief programmes were launched for Arab refugees supported by Churches from all over the world. Church World Service of the American Churches and the Lutheran World Federation carried out considerable food and medical operations in Asia and there were development projects in Korea. The extension of the mandate to include aid programmes anywhere in the world did not really develop until 1954 after the World Council second Assembly at Evanston, Illinois, U.S.A.

In 1952 the Mau Mau rebellion erupted in Kenya and terrible suffering and distress was prevalent throughout the colony. Mr. S. A. Morrison, a C.M.S. missionary in the Middle East for over twenty years, who for two years organised the refugee operation planned at the first World Council of Churches Beirut Conference in 1951, arrived in London in 1953. He was a highly educated and intelligent man, a good organiser and had a remarkable singleness of purpose about anything he set out to do. He had organised an impressive programme for the refugees and had encouraged the various Arab communities to set up working committees in each of the countries involved. He then began tentatively to discuss reconciliation between the two communities and before long he became *persona non grata* in Jordan where the majority of the Palestinian refugees were living. Within two days he and his wife were back in the United Kingdom.

The Christian Council of Kenya was basically a missionary council and some of its members, but not by any means all, were suspicious of the World Council of Churches. Its secretarial staff were 'volunteers' from the various missionary and Church organisations. When the revolt started they soon saw that they must plan immediately to take responsibility for as much of the desperately needed social programmes as possible. A full-time secretary was absolutely necessary and the Church Missionary Society suggested that Mr. Morrison should go out temporarily to help the Christian Council, which he did in the spring of 1954. Within a few weeks, the World Council of Churches in Geneva, the Conference of British Missionary Societies and Christian Aid (then called Inter-Church Aid) in Great Britian were bombarded daily with telegrams and express letters from Nairobi. Mr. Morrison was 'demanding' £50,000 in three months (to be raised to £100,000 by the end of the year) and at least a dozen specialised staff. None of us had that kind of money on hand. The World Council of Churches' Evanston Assembly was meeting in July and most of us 'at the receiving end' of Morrison's letters were there. I had to leave three months earlier because I was to be responsible for the dramatic presentation of the Inter-Church Aid evening and had to be there ahead of time to make the necessary preparations. Mr. Morrison was very angry. Very properly he thought our priorities were wrong and the human problems in Kenya much more urgent than a conference, however important.

One evening at Evanston, Dr. Leonard Beecher the Bishop of Mombasa, (now the Archbishop of East Africa) called a meeting outside the Assembly Hall to discuss what could be done to help Kenya. Dr. Robert Mackie, Director of the World Council of Churches Division of Inter-Church Aid, Canon M. A. C. Warren, General Secretary of the Church Missionary Society, Dr. J. W. C. McDougal of the Church of Scotland, Dr. Norman Goodall, a leading British Congregationalist, and I were present. It had already been arranged for me to go to the Middle East at Christmas to visit the refugee camps and Canon Warren suggested I should go on to Kenya and discuss the whole matter with Mr. Morrison, the Christian Council and other Church leaders in order to find out exactly what was needed. I was to report back to both the World and British Councils of Churches.

I had never been into a 'missionary' area before or to any other country outside Europe except the United States. I arrived one morning in January 1955 after an eighteen-hour night flight, tired and somewhat apprehensive. I was met by Mr. and Mrs. Morrison, taken to their home for a cup of tea, and there and then in their living-room, my luggage in the hall, we started on the minute by minute programme for the next fortnight. Two hours later, and after a bath and lunch, we set off on the first instalment and met the first group of leaders. The next day I was taken to visit some of the detainee camps and prisons. It was pouring with rain. I'll never forget those detainee camps. Hundreds and hundreds of African men huddled together in groups in large wire-netting compounds, with grey blankets held tightly round their bodies. The grey sky, the grey faces and the grey blankets made them all look like L. S. Lowry's paintings which are so popular today, almost 'stick' men, unhappy and lost. I found it hard to take. They were men. What were they feeling and thinking? Guards with guns were at every entrance and the officers in charge, mostly 'nice' men, were worried and harassed, but efficient.

Those involved in the Mau Mau outbreak were chiefly from the one and a quarter million Kikuyu, including small numbers from the Luo and other tribes. Some ten per cent of the Kikuyu had resisted when asked to take the first Mau Mau oath, among them being many Christians who had suffered martyrdom. The taking of primitive oaths of varying intensity was compulsory for all involved in the revolt, and many who refused were killed. There were approximately eighty thousand in detainee camps and prisons. The basic problem in Kenya before the emergency which the Churches had had to face was not so much one of hatred between Africans and Europeans, but of indifference. Very few knew how the other community actually lived. The multi-racial society desired by the British could only come about when sufficient people on both sides really wanted to get to know one another but communication was extremely difficult. The emergency had produced three major problems. First, the massive one arising from a revolution taking place in urban areas, where a new African industrial population faced bewildering adjustments in habit patterns of life; secondly the basic needs of Africans who had been collected from the scattered single homesteads to which they were accustomed and established in hastily erected villages, and thirdly the needs for social work in detainee camps and prisons. The Churches in Kenya did not ask for aid to strengthen the normal work of the missions, which had been disrupted, but the hospitals and other institutions were in great demand. What was required was social services and personal welfare for the present emergency. The major problem was the transition of a whole people from one pattern of life to another in the midst of the horrors and disillusionment caused by the Mau Mau outbreak. How the emergency was met in the next few years would be crucial for the future of Kenya, and hence also for the future evolution of similar problems elsewhere in Africa. In this situation of human need the Churches must themselves learn and grasp how to demonstrate the vital contribution Africa would make to the world.

After innumerable visits to prisons all over a large part of Kenya, long discussions with Church leaders and meetings with the Christian Council produced a first list of needs, both of money and workers.

BACKGROUND OF A REVOLUTION

Following military operations large numbers of Kikuyu were detained in camps, and the colonial government felt the urgent need to try and change the outlook of the detainees and encourage them to renounce Mau Mau. It was difficult for the Government and the European population to recognise Mau Mau as a violent protest against colonial rule and a declaration, however vile in form, of the people to be independent. They had lost their patience.

Kikuyu normally lived in isolated hamlets. For security reasons it became necessary to bring them into villages. This had been a major change in their way of life and brought problems of adjustment, both psychological and physical, especially in health, education, recreation and social relationships. But it provided possibilities for the people and the Churches wanted to take this opportunity to serve the people. Since so many men were detained and away from home, there was a need to concentrate on training the women, because as the men returned the families would need help to resettle. The needs of youth in these new surroundings were urgent and the care of children was essential. Nairobi was the centre of the Mau Mau organisation. The social structure of the African sections of the city of Nairobi was changing, and the churches in Kenya were invited to enter this field of service and willingly accepted.

After my return Christian Aid decided to raise £100,000 in 1955 and 1956 for projects planned. This was to help sponsor the opening of five community centres in the urban areas of Nairobi, to undertake the organisation of special work among women and youth, to train African workers for rehabilitation work in the newly established villages, to provide mobile units to visit villages and camps with literature and general teaching equipment, to provide social workers for the camps and prisons and to train Christian leaders.

By 1955 approximately £40,000 was raised in Great Britain and eight European workers and forty Africans were recruited. During the year, with help from the local authority, work was begun on the building of five community centres in Nairobi. By the end of the year four were completed and opened. Although special work for children had not been included in the original programme, it became clear early in the operation that there was a great need for work to be done among the large number of orphaned and neglected children. A large home was opened at Dagoretti to house five hundred children in need of care. The Government provided the building, the local authority provided maintenance and the Christian Council of Kenya undertook to staff and run the home. The full complement of five hundred children were soon settled. Attached to the Children's Centre there was a training course for 'home visitors'. It was hoped that ultimately two hundred and eighty African women would have attended this course. One woman was selected from each village, and after training it was hoped that they would go back and pass on what they had learnt to the other women in their villages. One European worker, a trained midwife, was touring the villages and trying to open and supervise infant welfare centres.

Youth leadership courses and summer schools were introduced and three African married couples were trained for work in the new resettlement villages in the

Mwea Plain. Their object was to help the former detainees and their families in their adjustment to the new conditions facing them in the resettlement villages. One mobile unit was donated. Two European and thirteen African workers were engaged in special rehabilitation work in the detention camps and prisons. Appreciation of their contribution to the spiritual rehabilitation of the prisoners has been frequently expressed by the highest authorities.

Eventually the £100,000 was raised in the British Isles and, while the United States sent food and some money, in the main it was a British effort. The first part of the appeal was jointly done by Christian Aid and those British missionary societies with work in Kenya.

Since then I have been to Kenya nine times, the last time being in 1967. When I was there in 1961 the atmosphere was very different. Plans were well in hand for Independence and the Christian Council of Kenya was a very different organisation.

In 1961 John Kamau, a Kikuyu, was appointed General Secretary and I went to discuss the phasing out by 1970 of Christian Aid's 'emergency' programmes started in 1955. Now, in collaboration with the Government, they were concerned with long-term development programmes. The staff are almost all African and the work of the Council is entirely in the hands of Africans. An ecumenical newspaper, in collaboration with the Tanzania Christian Council, flourishes, edited at first by Stanley Booth Clibborn who was recruited during the emergency, and industrial trade schools; home industries and other social programmes are still at work. We had also sent £100,000 to help with higher education and this has opened doors to further extension of educational programmes.

My last visit was in 1967 and as well as discussing extension to the agricultural projects I was at a refugee and emergency committee of the Emergency Programme for Ecumenical Action in Africa. I visited the Ruanda refugees and other groups. There they were, a symbol of this century of the homeless men. But Kenya flourishes. It has its problems of unemployment in the urban areas and many other needs but it 'feels' stable and buoyant and all hope this will continue to be the case.

During these years I have several times visited many other parts of Africa, and Christian Aid was involved in a large number of enterprises in Tanzania, Uganda, Central Africa, Rhodesia and West Africa. So many long-term development programmes in Africa started as post-emergency or civil war relief. The first major emergency was the Congo but on the whole this description of the Kenya revolt indicates the united action taken in all similar emergencies. We were glad that British Christian Aid had the opportunity to be in at the beginning of widespread ecumenical social programmes in many parts of Africa.

5

MEMORIES FROM JOURNEYS

MEMORIES FROM JOURNEYS

I MADE many journeys all over the world during the years with Christian Aid. Most of them were for the World Council of Churches, but those to Kenya and the Middle East were often at the request of the Christian Aid Board. Some of the reports and diaries have disappeared, but looking through those I have they present a saga of world human problems that I have seen with my own eyes in many parts of the world. Here are some extracts. By their very nature some will need to be longer than others. In previous chapters you will have read of some schemes that developed from what I saw as a 'professional' traveller.

JACKSON, MISSISSIPPI

I arrived in Jackson, Mississippi, U.S.A., on the 6th October 1965, and was met by the Reverend Bob Beech and the Reverend Bruce Hilton, both staff members of the Delta Ministry. We went to a café for a meal and they immediately made me feel I was one of the team. I felt that throughout the eleven days I stayed with them. I felt as though I had never been anywhere else, and that I was there for good. I realised at the end that it was partly because of the united single-mindedness of all the staff and volunteers, and also because they were involved every minute of their lives with the basic tragedies of human life.

HATTIESBURG

That night and the next I stayed in Hattiesburg with Mr. and Mrs. Beech and their three children. The Reverend R. Beech is the Director of the Delta Ministry project in Hattiesburg. He has been there two years and is a Presbyterian Minister.

In 1963 the Commissions on Religion and Race of the National Council of Churches and the United Presbyterian Church of the United States prepared for the 'Hattiesburg Minister Project'. This was the result of an appeal made for ministers to go to Hattiesburg and help the Negroes to register for voting. Changing laws made the conditions for voting more possible, but Negroes had to be encouraged to vote. They were frightened because of the persecution so many had endured because they had gone to register, and yet to change the structure of society so that 'all men are equal' it is necessary to be registered for voting. Over fifty ministers went for various periods in 1964 and paved the way for the Delta Ministry, which started in October of that year.

The Negroes need encouragement to get over their fears and go through with the hazards of actually going to the appropriate office to register. The questions on the forms, which I would have been unable to answer, were very difficult and of a legal character and black voters needed coaching. Since then as a result of massive representation the forms have been composed of simpler questions. Often the fact of taking what to us is a simple right as a citizen meant losing a poorly paid job with no further prospects available.

The Mississippi Delta Ministry was a year old when I arrived. There were fourteen staff members, a mixture of whites and Negroes. Six were Mississippians. Over Five hundred volunteers had helped during the year. They came from all over the United States. The National Council of Churches of the United States did not plan to impose a 'Northern' organisation on the Mississippi. The Delta Ministry is run by the Mississippi people, and the staff and volunteers help them. This is not an academic statement. I sat on many committees and visited Negro homes and talked to their leaders, and the impressive thing was the way the Delta Ministry staff stayed 'silent' in meetings and took a back seat when decisions were made.

IN ITS FIRST YEAR, THE DELTA MINISTRY

... played a major part in the registration of 10,000 new Negro voters in four counties ... helped bring 'Head Start' schools to Mississippi over the violent objection of racist politicians in the state; this gave 1,100 summer jobs to Negroes and a pre-school boost to nearly 6,000 youngsters ... supported a doctor and four nurses in a county health improvement programme ... in co-operation with the National Student Association and the Department of Agriculture, offered to distribute government surplus food in eighteen counties which had no such welfare programme; the counties rushed to set up their own programmes and thousands more poor people ate better as a result ... conducted citizenship workshops and seminars all over the state to train enlightened voters and skilled leaders ... distributed tons of food and clothing, through local committees which assessed the need, to approximately 10,000 families ... supported local employment committees fighting job discrimination in four cities ... supported cotton-field workers in their efforts to get a better wage; when twelve such workers were forcibly evicted and found all rental housing closed to them, arranged for temporary housing and continues to support the strikers in their attempts to achieve human dignity.

POVERTY AND IMPRISONMENT

There is very great poverty among the Negroes and pre-school education is essential if the children are to measure up to integrated schools when it really becomes a fact. A Negro woman said to me, 'Ten children in a 600 school is not integration.' But it will come. I was told in Natches by a Negro about their inferior education. He said, 'Ignorance keeps young people from knowing the outside world. A Negro gets an inferior education then goes to an inferior Negro college and all he can do is to be a teacher in an inferior Negro school. Inferior all the way.'

It is this second-class citizenship, a fundamental insult to human dignity, that the Negroes are fighting. In some places it is now the law that cafés, swimming pools and buses are integrated. In Greenville where I stayed, part of the time in a Negro household, the town simply closed all the pools and took the buses off the road.

'WHITE NIGGERS'

The National Council of Churches has been criticised and had support withdrawn. Those taking part in the project are called communists, 'White Niggers' and 'trash'—a word that is much more insulting than it is in this country. The White members of the Delta Ministry staff are almost isolated in the places where they live. They decided they would all live in the white communities, and every possible legal and illegal method has been used to prevent them getting houses. They have been shot at, described in the papers as 'scum', and coldly received in shops and churches.

The amazing thing to me about the Negroes is their devotion to their faith and their Church. I wonder how long that will continue to be true. The whole Civil Rights Movement in Mississippi and other Southern States is rooted in the Negro Churches, and to attend a freedom rally, which I did, in a church, was to me a revelation. Now the young black people, while still greatly influenced by the Church background, feel it is irrelevant and are working in other organisations. It was very little different from the service I had attended the previous Sunday morning in another Baptist church. The speaker urged non-violence, implored the young people to stay at school as long as they could, and appealed for 'good and moral living.' This was all interspersed with sermons, biblical quotations, hymn-singing, good humour and terrible stories told by those who had been in prison, where they suffered physical and mental torture.

The American Churches asked the World Council of Churches to recognise the Delta Ministry as an ecumenical project. They said, 'This is something Christians everywhere must be concerned about. We are all in it together.' Christian Aid is in it also. So many of their problems are ours in this country.

The response was immediately positive. The Negro Christians need to know that, whoever else might be sympathetic to them, Christians all over the world are helping with their prayers and practical aid. The Delta Ministry is a 'Christian presence' in a horrifying situation. It only seeks to be with these suffering people in their time of travail. The work is organised by the Negro communities themselves, but the presence of Americans from other parts of the United States sent by the Churches is most impressive.

Mrs. Harmer, a remarkable Negro woman who, under different circumstances, would be a member of Congress, said to me: 'They carried me into a room and there was two Negro boys in this room. The state highway patrolman gave them a long, wide blackjack and he told one of the boys, "Take this," and the Negro, he said, "This what you want me to use?" The state patrolman said, "That's right, and if you don't use it on her you know what I'll use on you."

'I had to get over on a bed flat on my stomach and that man beat me . . . that man beat me till he give out. And by me screamin', it made a plain-clothes man—he didn't have on nothin' like a uniform—he got so hot and worked up he just run there and started hittin' me on the back of my head. And I was tryin' to guard some of the licks with my hands and they just beat my hands till they turned blue. This Negro just beat me till I know he was give out. Then this state patrolman told the other Negro to take me so he take over from there and he just keep beatin' me.'

I spent an evening with Mrs. Harmer and she said, 'I'm sick and tired of being sick and tired.

'We're tired of all this beatin', we're tired of takin' this. It's been a hundred years and we're still being beaten and shot at, crosses are still being burned, because we want to vote. But I'm goin' to stay in Mississippi and if they shoot me down, I'll be buried here. But I don't want equal rights with the white man, if I did, I'd be a thief and a murderer. But the white man is the scaredest person on earth. Out in the daylight he don't do nothin'—But at night he'll toss a bomb or pay someone to kill. The white man's afraid he'll be treated like he's been treatin' Negroes, but I couldn't carry that much hate. It wouldn't solve any problem for me to hate whites just because they hate me. Oh, there's so much hate. Only God has kept the Negro sane.'

As I left her home late one night she said, 'This is a battle with the Church in the front line; I am proud to be on the Delta Ministry Committee.' 'We mustn't hate——' 'When I was in prison they visited me.' One of her famous sayings is, 'I'm sick and tired of being sick and tired.' 'I may be murdered—but we must fight on.'

During my stay there I spent some time with Vernon Dahmer, a good humble man longing for peace and justice. This is what happened to him.

On the 10th January, 1966, at two o'clock in the morning, Vernon Dahmer, the Negro member of the staff of the 'Delta Ministry', was startled out of his sleep by the sound of shooting. He wanted to run to the door, but his face was covered with splintered glass. Then there was an explosion in the entrance-hall. He fetched his wife, his two sons and his daughter, and hurried to the door again. He was met by a rain of bullets. Vernon Dahmer got his rifle and shot back, while his family escaped through the window. The next day he died in the Negro section of the local hospital from the wounds and burns he had received. He died, while four of his grown-up sons were fighting in the American Army for the freedom of the West. He died, not because he had demonstrated but because he had placed his house at the disposal of the 'Delta Ministry' for teaching Negro children and adults. He died because he had allowed his house to be used for distributing food and clothing to the cold, hungry Negroes, and because in his house Negroes had been taught how to get their names included on the lists of voters as citizens with full rights. He died knowing that no insurance company had accepted the risk of insuring his house, because it was the house of an 'extremist'.

It would be a mistake to imagine that such cases are properly dealt with by the legal system in Mississippi and in the other Southern States of America. The evil-doers are not punished at all.

A CHANGING SOCIETY

It was a unique experience for me to visit the cotton fields. I found nothing romantic about the Negro shacks, such as my story book *Uncle Tom's Cabin* led me to believe when I was a child. They are broken-down poverty-stricken rat-ridden wooden huts. Most of the families have lived in them since their grandparents were 'freed' from slavery.

Great economic changes are taking place. Most of the cotton is now picked by machinery and, while some owners allow the families to stay in their shacks, great social changes are in process. I saw fields where all the picking was done by hand, but the majority is done by machines. Pickers are needed for the ends of the rows where the machines can't penetrate. The Negroes get two dollars a day for picking and the machine-drivers six dollars.

Some Negroes are share-croppers. This means they are on a fifty-fifty basis with the owners but the Negroes have to provide all the seeds, fertilisers and labour out of their fifty per cent. There is little left and what there is he has to 'spend' at stores owned by his owner, and the Negro is always in debt to him. Whatever the outcome of the race question there will be a tremendous unemployment problem in the next few years. The Negro has no economic future. Crowds of Negroes are going North where there are so-called liberal laws, but segregation is to all intents and purposes almost complete.

There is not space to report all the tragic and moving consultations I had with those who had suffered violence. I sat in small shops and houses and listened to tragic stories told me in a language Shakespearian in style, and I cannot find words to describe their courtesy and dignity as they spoke of their Christian faith and their struggle for social justice. Even the young people who speak less frequently of their faith are conscious of their Church roots, and all believe that true Christians should stand for social justice.

SINGING AND PROTESTING

Everywhere the Negroes sing and meetings always start and finish with songs about themselves and their struggle. I shall never forget singing 'We shall overcome' linked together at the end of every meeting, or in various houses before going home. Since then 'We shall overcome' has become a world-wide protest song, but I find it difficult to stomach when it is sung at a football match or a minor protest staged for superficial reasons.

I visited Mississippi again in December 1968 and stayed in Mrs. Harmer's village. While there were signs of improvement the poverty was as before. This time except for those of us from outside all the people at meetings were black. Now, generally speaking except for the over-forty middle-class group, 'Negro' is not acceptable. Black is beautiful. In January 1970 I watched Mrs. Harmer on B.B.C. Television in my sitting-room in a programme about discrimination in the United States—still in fighting form.

FAMINE

In 1961 I made my first prolonged visit to Nigeria and as well as visiting briefly other parts of Africa I returned home by Kenya, Tanganyika and Uganda. It must have been my sixth or seventh visit to Kenya. While we were still supporting a considerable programme in Kenya, started in 1954 during the Mau Mau revolution, it was on that visit that I talked with the Christian Council of Kenya about our involvement in the Freedom From Hunger Campaign. The outcome was the seven projects mentioned elsewhere. My notes of that visit hardly do credit to the famine problem of the time.

'There were parts of Kenya suffering very greatly from famine, not only in the Lokitaung area but also in Nakuru and Rift Valley. We also heard about the famine problems of the Masai tribe. We were told of large areas where cattle were lying dead in the fields and I saw mounds of carcases on the roadside. It was said that in one area there had been no rain for three years, and in some places four hundred cattle were dying each month. It was decided to set up a committee to be called 'The Relief, Research and Resettlement Committee', which would deal with emergency feeding first and then a long-term programme of a pilot nature. The Government had introduced a yeoman farmers' scheme planning to re-settle them in the Rift Valley. In this area there were at least 200,000 unemployed. If the famine continued there would be more. The Bishop of Nakuru had put forward an imaginative scheme which the Committee considered. The Committee hoped to provide us with an overall scheme in the near future which would probably include a request for some expert help during the planning period. They would be working closely with the Government.'

You will have already read that in the Freedom from Hunger Campaign Christian Aid raised half a million pounds to develop this programme.

In Tanganyika the ugly word 'famine' came up again. We discussed all kinds of medical, agricultural and community-centre projects which we eventually supported from Christian Aid and also provided personnel. But the immediate needs were to put bread into hungry mouths.

Some areas are badly affected by famine. The Government is providing food, the people having been put into camps. The clergy and ministers are paid by the congregations, but because of the famine they are too poor at present to contribute anything. There is real distress among these pastors. If they could be provided with essential resources they could assist with welfare as well as giving spiritual encouragement in the camps.

It was agreed to ask the Standing Committee of the Christian Council to set up a project committee to prepare a list for the World Council of Churches and Christian Aid would support it up to the hilt.

UGANDA

My first engagement in Uganda was to visit Mrs. Sabin, the Mayor of Kampala, a very energetic woman involved in much social work in Uganda, and Chairman of the Y.W.C.A. She spoke of the need for hostels for young people in the hope that Christian Aid and the World Council would soon begin to support agricultural and community development projects as Uganda was approaching independence and was all set for development. She said that youth work was a priority because there is much unemployment and juvenile delinquency. Young people are pouring into Kampala and living in the most appalling places. She also spoke of the need for agricultural programmes and mentioned the work of the Y.W.C.A. in this respect. Eighty-six per cent of the agriculture in the country depends upon the woman and she was hoping that the Y.W.C.A. would plan courses for women all over the country, including training for better husbandry, integration of stock, nutrition lectures, better feeding, improved farm planning, marketing and harvesting. She promised to ask the Y.W.C.A. in Geneva to let me have a scheme as soon as it could be planned. The Mayor stressed the need for a school of social studies, for the training of those who would never receive higher education. The previous year the Mayor was an African; this year a European and next year it would be an Asian.

Later in the morning I was taken to the home of the Reverend Asa Byara, who lives on the Naguru housing estate; he has no building except his house in which to do all his church and pastoral work. He is an excellent person and full of ideas. He and Archdeacon Butler of Jinja had been to a Conference at Limuru in Kenya and he had come back full of enthusiasm and immediately prepared projects designed to help people now living in new housing areas as well as in the slums of Kampala. He says what is true of many places in Africa, that the Church in urban areas is in many ways like an extension of the village Church working in the village patterns, using village methods in its ministry to an urban community. He said that this is quite an impossible situation.

There were about 70,000 Africans working or living in Kampala and they come from as many as forty-two tribes, and about 24,000 Africans who actually live within the municipal boundary. There is only one church and very few other organisations doing social work. The cathedral and churches adjacent to the town do not cater for the mass of people either living in housing areas or in terrible slums. He quoted a Roman Catholic Bishop who said that 'today the emphasis has changed and changed so abruptly that there is danger that it may be missed until it is too late, and it is in the townships where the new leaders of Africa dwell'.

I also visited some quite dreadful slums accompanied by Miss Vera Morton, an English woman who is helping Mr. Byara in his work, and Mr. Kalanzi, the head chief working under the Kabaka. He, an Anglican layman, is very distressed about the social conditions. He took me to the Kibuga area, which has a population of 23,000 with no church or social centre, and where at least seventeen tribes are represented. Obviously there was very great poverty and much unemployment. What it needs is 'honest to goodness social work' carried out by Africans. Another bad area we visited was Kisenyi, again over 20,000 population with no facilities, but here there are plans for improvement. An old building has been found which they hope will be turned into a sort of social settlement and there is already an African social worker in charge. The Dulverton Trust of the United Kingdom has given them £17,000 to alter the building, and a special Trustees Committee has been set up for this social centre called Nakivubo. There is also a school in this area which is used by the Y.W.C.A. in the evenings for classes for girls. Evening classes have already been started in the main building which is still in a derelict condition. We visited other places including Ketwe and Nsambya Hill, both depressing townships, all in need of social centres. Two years later I laid the foundation stone of a community centre in a suburb of Kampala.

As before, it was possible to provide considerable help for all these projects as they developed.

My general comments at the end of a long report included some paragraphs that are still very relevant in Africa.

While there are very real differences in the cultural and social life of the four countries I visited, there are certain common problems and aspirations facing both State and Church. As the countries and the Churches become independent their requests for outside support are, generally speaking, similar in character. This is probably true of other countries in Africa and many countries in Asia.

The first and most important problem is endemic poverty. In the excitement of preparing or consolidating the emergence into new nationhood this major task facing governments can easily be overlooked by the outside world which is preoccupied with terrifying international problems of peace and war. A good deal of the poverty is not real starvation. The number of people who die of starvation in a dramatic way must be very small, but under-feeding has a long-term devastating effect on an individual. To be consistently under-fed—such food as is available is usually deficient in balance and sustenance—is an insidious enemy, not only to life expectation but also to political and social development.

The second common concern is the need to develop an indigenous political philosophy. Inevitably the process will be influenced by the outgoing colonial government. The difference between the approach to politics of an African from Nigeria and one from the French Cameroun is the difference between the British and French attitudes to political life. It is useless at any rate in the immediate future for other nations seeking to sell 'their way of life' to African nations to disregard this, because the African nations in their desire to flower into sophisticated political entities can only start from what they know. This is not essentially a bad thing, but it will be tragic if they are forced to accept offers of economic aid with hidden political strings attached, either from the East or the West, before they have time to begin to develop independent political maturity. As African countries become, by sheer numbers, a power in the United Nations, the temptation to sell their political souls to the highest bidder will be tremendous. The recent tragic war situations in many countries having achieved independence demonstrates this deep-seated problem in a fast-changing world.

The third problem common to all is the danger that in moving from one particular kind of colonialism they will perforce take on the mantle of another. This is a real dilemma because of the necessity to tackle endemic poverty, to deal with the need for education, and the immediate necessity to secure economic stability.

The fourth and perhaps most important common concern is the search for spiritual security. This is the most difficult to articulate. The different tribal cultures to be found in each country and the variety of religions and superstitions, are inevitably in conflict with one another as each nation struggles to find national unity. The fact that in every country there is only a small number of educated and sophisticated politicians places a tremendous responsibility on a few leaders, thereby widening the gap between them and the uneducated masses. This is not peculiar to African nations, but those outside wishing to help by providing food and other basic physical necessities must at least understand this equally important human need. I believe that the Churches are appealing for help because they are aware of these fundamental needs and they are only too conscious of their lack of resources. I found in conversations with African Christians in all four countries that they are united with their non-Christian brothers in their passionate desire for political independence on their own terms. Most of those I met are impatient at the apparent lack of unity among Christians and look to the World Council of Churches for guidance as they seek to draw closer to each other.

If Christian Aid is able to help the Churches in their increasing responsibility, all concerned must be sensitive to these very human personal and political problems and the accompanying aspirations.

I had the feeling when I went round a department store in Lagos that commerce with all its paraphernalia of advertising and 'togetherness' would do more in changing social behaviour than serious-minded Western and African sociologists might imagine.

Since I wrote this there have been civil wars and revolutions in some of those countries, and the prospects are that there will be more, but the human problems remain.

HONG KONG IN 1968

'Flying into Hong Kong for the first time was like being transported into fairyland. I stayed there six weeks at the request of the World Council of Churches Refugee Committee, of which I was Chairman. The rocky and mountainous islands, the brilliant blue of the sea and sky, the purple shadows on the hillsides, are almost too much to grasp at first sight. The picturesque sampans dipping up and down in the sea and the beauty of line of the peaceful-looking warships in the harbour are so like a too-brilliant picture postcard that it is almost unbelievable. Then the blaze of oriental colour of even the most ordinary domestic signs in the streets of Kowloon and Hong Kong dazzles the Westerner's eyes accustomed to opaque colours and a milk and watery conception of a city landscape. Reading my Report twelve years later, during which time I returned to Hong Kong several times, recalls to my mind a poverty the like of which I had never seen before.

A later impression is quite different: so many people that it is impossible to move about without physically touching humanity as you pass by. It will not be easy to forget the exotic colour and beauty nor yet the overwhelming impression of acquiescent humanity in the mass. The crowds of children lining up with rice bowls for supplementary feeding, squalid homes in cardboard shacks on roof-tops and thousands living on the pavements almost wipe out the memory of the beauty of Hong Kong. The vast government resettlement blocks, six or seven storeys high, brightly coloured and contemporary in design, stand out as modern symbols of the forced gregariousness of this century of the refugee and homeless people. There are small rooms, narrow corridors, back streets, all packed with people, and shops of all sizes everywhere. It seems as though seventy-five per cent of the population runs a business of some kind or other. Fancy? Perhaps, but there are a large number of street markets and little businesses typical, I was told, of a Chinese population.

In 1931 the population of Hong Kong was 849,751. It is now estimated to be three million, ninety per cent of whom are Chinese. The population during these years has fluctuated greatly. In 1938, during the hostilities between China and Japan, large numbers of refugees fled into the Colony, so that in 1941 the population had risen to about one and a half million. Hong Kong was occupied by the Japanese in 1942 and by the end of the occupation in 1945 the population was reduced to half a million. Since that time, as a result of civil war in China, the return of Hong Kong residents who left during the occupation and the continuing influx of immigrants from the mainland have resulted in the present estimated population of three million. The total area of the Colony is 391 square miles with an overall density of 7,700 inhabitants per square mile but in certain places there are 2,000 and more per acre. One of the great dangers of the squatter areas on the hillsides of Hong Kong is fire and there have been many during the past seven years. At Christmas 1954 a catastrophic fire rendered 60,000 people homeless in one night. It was then that the Government, who had been postponing large building programmes, on the assumption that many of the immigrants from the mainland would return to their homes, decided to make a titanic effort to house the homeless and destitute. Their first plan was to build the resettlement blocks mentioned above.

It is quite remarkable that in spite of the overcrowding there has been no major epidemic. The nearest approach to one is the scourge of tuberculosis which is the most serious and urgent health problem. In one week in 1956 a seventh of the deaths from all causes were from T.B. It is the general opinion that at least seventy-five per cent of the population are in some way affected by tuberculosis. The need for more hospitals and medical staff is very great. Every effort is being made by the Government and the voluntary agencies to provide more hospital beds in order to relieve the overcrowded wards.

I was amazed at the extraordinary personal cleanliness of the majority of the people and the innate dignity shown in the face of such poverty and overcrowding.

While a small percentage of the refugees living in these areas and under such distressing conditions have been used to a more middle-class or intellectual way of life in China, the majority have come from very simple villages. The difference, of course, is that if you live in a shack in a village in the middle of a field your home is the open air with all the space of the earth and the sky about you, and your house is where you sleep and shelter from the sun and bad weather. These conditions, transferred to modern Western society, create a different social problem from the poverty of a village. The great gaps between wealth and poverty in Hong Kong are only too obvious.

The enormous building programme going on everywhere was very impressive. In order to carry this out it is necessary literally to move mountains, to reclaim large tracts of land from the sea and to excavate deep into the earth. The two previous occasions when I saw this mushroom building were in Germany immediately after the war when the Germans furiously rebuilt such cities as Hanover, Stuttgart and Dusseldorf and more recently in Israel where everybody seemed to be building something somewhere.

My impression was that the Churches in the main are 'respectable' and used by the better-dressed and more intelligent groups of the community. Here, as elsewhere, the Churches seem unable to catch the imagination of the mass of industrial workers. The increasing numbers of new converts appear to be drawn from the poor and needy who seek spiritual security as well as economic security.

Every conceivable voluntary and welfare organisation seems to be active in Hong Kong and most of them are in some way involved in the distribution of relief and the necessary rehabilitation programmes. The majority of the population are naturally non-Christian and all live in a tolerant society where, as long as they do not break the peace, 'anything goes'. Black market, drugs, political underground activity, are a few of the snares for the young entrants into Hong Kong of whatever nationality.

There is no doubt that the Government has done an

excellent and imaginative job in trying to rehouse the homeless, not only in the resettlement areas but in the better type of housing also, and they have catered for the new generation by building many schools. New schooling is provided each year for 30,000 children. The natural increase of population each year is 75,000.

It needs to be remembered that it takes courage to carry out new building, economic development and welfare activity when the expectation of life for Hong Kong could be forty years, one year or even one week. Who knows?

Since then conditions have greatly improved. Refugees still come and there have been riots. Christian Aid has provided very large sums of money and people to help with that enormous problem of human need.

DIARY OF A SOUTH-EAST ASIA TOUR IN 1959

'I had a comfortable and fast journey on the Comet IV, arriving in Karachi just about half an hour late.

'The next morning, before going on to Lahore, I took a taxi and did a tour of the city. This lasted for an hour. I found the city strangely weary and old. Going down Victoria Road and past the Museum Gardens I thought it almost pathetic to see the slightly battered statue of Queen Victoria standing alone, all dignity departed.

'It was intriguing to be in a foreign country and driving on the left. I was also interested to see that the jerry-built lorries were being pulled by old, seedy-looking camels. There was a great use of donkeys, and in one place where the road was being built, the donkeys were in the hole where the men were digging and putting the soil into bags strapped on to the donkeys' backs. This was all mixed up with large fast-driven American cars and evidence of a wealthy element in a city of very poor people. There was great expansion going on in Karachi; more new, high-class houses and more large office buildings. A vast area on the beach is being turned into a deluxe hotel which is being built by an American firm. It will include a theatre, a swimming pool and all modern amenities. Fifty per cent of the shareholdings will be in the hands of the Pakistani Government, twenty-five per cent in the hands of the oil company and twenty-five per cent in the hands of the American company. Foreign money is pouring into Pakistan, particularly from the United States. This was, I thought, true of everywhere in Pakistan; ninety per cent of the population is Muslim.'

I was met at Lahore by Feodor and Elsa Peter, with whom I stayed, the excellent Swiss brother and sister who are doing such good work among refugees in rural areas. He is an engineer and carried out on behalf of the Government important experiments on land bedevilled by salt and new forms of irrigation.

In 1948, when nine or ten million refugees were crossing the border, it was quite clear that something had to be done for the women, and a Pakistani headmistress of a girls' school, Mrs. Marjory Paul, gave up teaching and gathered women together in groups. She found that they needed to do something constructive whereby they could be trained to earn their living, She was joined by Miss Peter. I saw the first group of women in a top room in a poor part of the city of Lahore. They were divided into three groups; older women were doing hem-stitching round pieces of embroidery; apparently, these women in the very beginning were very simple and unused to using their fingers, and were only able to make paper bags which they sold to the shops, but now Mrs. Paul has taught them how to do very skilled hem-stitching, and it is impossible to tell that it has not been done by machine. There were younger women actually doing the embroidery. The third group was comprised of children who were being taught English and writing, and in another room there was another group of women who were just learning the stitches. Other groups knitted children's garments. After training most of them became highly skilled and professional, earning money for their families. The village women were the only family breadwinners because there was no work for the men. These women are from lower-middle-class homes, one or two of them married but mostly unmarried. It is quite clear that this occupation has given them a new attitude to life. While they are there each day from eight o'clock in the morning until four in the afternoon, they get food and milk, most of which is made from the dried milk sent by the American Churches. Miss Peter told me that you could see daily the improvement of their health, the result of the regular milk diet. Their skins became brighter and they looked better in every way.

Most, but not all of the women from the twenty-nine villages are Christian and come in to Lahore at intervals for training and also to sell their goods. All the women in the town groups were Muslim. A shop had been opened in the best part of the city and there was a packing area where goods were being packed for export overseas. Their biggest overseas market is Canada, where the United Churchwomen of Canada, particularly the women's groups of the Episcopal Church in Canada have taken it up in a big way, and they can hardly meet the orders. It was the hope of Mr. and Miss Peter that other countries would take large quantities to sell. They did and there is now a considerable overseas market in many countries.

Later I visited a blind institution, the only one of its

kind in Pakistan. I was very impressed by Miss Fyson, the Englishwoman in charge. She is living quite alone with about twenty-five children and adolescents, all blind, teaching them to do most remarkable things. Up to now, nobody has cared about the blind, and they have lived a very miserable, poor and lonely existence. As well as helping a small number of children to live a fuller life, the pioneer project encourages the community at large to see the value as well as the human responsibility of caring for the blind.

Early one morning I was taken by colleagues to visit a remote West Pakistan village. This I regarded as important because it really gave me a picture of what rural life is like in Pakistan and India and the kind of work that the Church and other bodies are doing in the sub-continent. The village was mostly Muslim, with two or three Christian families. There was a school run by Christian teachers, a man and his wife, both village people who had been taken into the town and trained and then brought back to run their school. Highly intelligent people, who, if they had had the advantages of a city background or had come from a more educated family, would undoubtedly have gone far. It was extremely hot, 110°, with the sun beating down on to the houses made of mud and flattened cow dung. The houses I visited were clean, just one-roomed, with beds piled up and covered with brightly coloured material and all round the walls were basket-work trays and copper pots and aluminium pots of various kinds for domestic use. The school was in one of the houses, the various charts and books stored under the beds. Since that first visit, considerable quantities of the embroidery have been sold in Great Britain and funds have been provided for a number of development programmes.

CALCUTTA

After a sojourn in New Delhi I arrived at Calcutta at 8.30 p.m. on the 27th May and was met at the airport by Mr. and Mrs. Benedict, American relief workers. My first impression on the drive from the airport was of humanity and cows in the mass, both men and beasts lying about on the pavement or strolling in groups across the centre of the road. Walking about on the pavements means stepping over bodies or walking round cows. Cars blowing horns incessantly were ignored by all until the bonnets almost touched their shoulders, then people would step aside, and very slowly at that. I was most impressed by Mr. Benedict's skill in driving.

I had a fascinating three days because I was, for the first time, able to see refugees in India while in the past they had seemed almost a legend to me. Out of the eight million refugees that came from East Pakistan, over three million came to West Bengal, mostly to the Calcutta area. It is really true to speak of them as displaced persons and not refugees, for when they came at the time of Partition, eleven years ago, most of them were Hindu and Pakistan was a Muslim state. The population has been particularly difficult for West Bengal because more Muslims crossed from East Pakistan than from other parts of India, and so there was no available land or housing. The Government has done a tremendous job: about half a million have been rehabilitated in the resettlement sense of the word, but not economically rehabilitated. The West Bengal Government has created about four hundred refugee colonies. Those refugees coming into rural areas have been given a plot of land and money to build a small house—a prefabricated house of brick with one room. To some, grants have been given to start small businesses, but this has mostly been in urban areas. Also in urban areas, money has been given to build houses and grants for anything that would seem to rehabilitate refugees. Aid was also given to industrial organisations on condition that they employ refugees. All this happened at a time when the Government was trying to raise the standard of living for India generally. As India has, in the main, the largest underfed community in the world, the refugees have created a major problem. There are uncountable numbers of underfed, extremely poor people in India, and in one sense, I saw more endemic 'passive' hunger in Calcutta than I have seen anywhere else in the world. The advent of independence has caused psychological problems among the refugees—they rely all the time on the Government, and find it difficult to start to do things for themselves.

I visited three of the colonies and saw the pathetic squatters round the Sealdah station.

The Anglo-Indians are in an extremely difficult position. A special committee set up by the National Christian Council of India has just completed a survey and will make an effort to follow it up on the results. There is in existence an Anglo-Indian Association with branches in the various states; they are Christian, about two-thirds of whom are Roman Catholic. There are 30,000 Anglo-Indians in West Bengal. A few are still in good positions and live a good life but most of the educated Anglo-Indians left for the United Kingdom, Australia, Canada and the United States at the time of partition. The majority are desperately poor, there are some terrible slums, and many people are living in the most deplorable conditions.

They are a proud people, and have always had to fight against being regarded as a second-class community both by Indians and Europeans, and yet many distinguished people have emerged from that community. Their major problem is education and vocational training. Those who feel India is their home and wish to stay there and to survive must be better trained, better qualified and better educated than anybody else in order to obtain jobs and places in training centres because the competition is so great.

WHAT DO YOU KNOW ABOUT HUNGER?

The pot is boiling because somebody makes it boil.
                                        African proverb.

On a dark and icy cold morning in January 1946 I flew in an R.A.F. plane from Berlin to Kiel and then drove in a jeep to a British Army Church House a few miles outside the city. We passed through what had been the city centre but now the main street was a narrow, bumpy lane and the sides piled up with rubble. All round us were stark-naked ruins and such people as there were about were white-faced and grim. A man was searching in the filth for cigarette ends. Outside the city we passed by a refugee camp where white-faced, unsmiling boys and girls gazed at us through the railings. The next morning I looked out of the window of my warm bedroom into the backyard and saw a child enter the open gate from the garden, look cautiously round, lift the lid from an overflowing garbage bin and quickly and efficiently pick out the scraps of bread and other left-overs from our supper tables the previous night. She ran off with breakfast for her respectable middle-class family. I have never forgotten that little girl. This was what war had done to innocent children, not only had it starved them of food but reduced them to be scavengers.

I thought of her in 1955 when I was in Kenya at the height of the Mau Mau and saw hungry children huddled in corners of African huts. They were afraid of us until we managed to reassure them. Their parents had been taken off to detainee camps, and they were lonely and desolate. She came into my mind when a woman in the slums of West Kingston, Jamaica, with a child at her breast and another three hanging around her skirts followed me around for two hours repeating, 'some milk would be better than nothing'.

She was there again when I helped in a feeding centre in Seoul in Korea, when the people came from broken-down shacks once a day to get soup and rice. Walking about at night in the streets of Calcutta and of necessity stepping over emaciated bodies too lethargic to move, or visiting refugee shacks in beautiful Hong Kong, or standing helplessly in the filthy slums of Kampala, always the same agony and anger assailed me as it did on that cold morning in Kiel. I asked myself each time, why can't I make the pot boil? It is easy for a well-fed English-woman like myself to shake with anger about the futility of war, to protest verbally about the iniquity of racial prejudice and to deplore the helplessness of little people in the face of vast political forces fighting for power. It is less easy to take a full share of the blame and almost impossible to understand the feelings and aspirations of the legions of hungry people in the world.

I know nothing about hunger. I thought of that little girl last week when I nibbled some chocolates at a London theatre. The price of those chocolates would have paid for food for an Indian family for one day.

WE WERE FORCED TO OPEN A CLINIC

On Sunday, 10th January 1965, I left Enugu, Eastern Nigeria, where I was attending World Council of Churches meetings, to drive eighty miles to Echara to see the Rural Improvement Mission which has received so much valuable support from the people of Cardiff. I was driven by an agriculturalist Mr. Bob Burke, an Irish C.M.S. Missionary, and we were accompanied by two World Council staff members. We descended on the 'Hutchison household' in the early afternoon. Mr. and Mrs. Hutchison and their four children live in a small house and we received a warm welcome and much-needed cold drinks. As we looked through the open windows at the few small buildings scattered around Mr. Hutchison said:

'We were forced to open a clinic. We had hardly been here a few hours before a queue of women started to form on the assumption that we would provide them with medical care. They took no notice when we explained that we were primarily concerned with agricultural development—they just kept coming. How could we turn them away? Now we have those two small buildings and we serve nearly 800 people a month and provide transport to take the serious cases to the nearest hospital twenty miles away.'

This is typical of the whole operation and I wish the subscribers from Cardiff could go and see the project.

BAGS OF RICE

In the little clinic which has a few beds we saw three mothers with their minute twins being nursed to life.

One woman was so undernourished that she had to have special care for some weeks. Cheek by jowl with the clinic was a rice store with a large number of hundredweight bags of rice ready to take to the nearest town market. Then we went a mile or two down the road to one of the four land development schemes. Nine eager-faced young men were lined up waiting for us. In 1962 when Mr. Hutchison was working for the Presbyterian Church of Nigeria he decided to open up work in Echara which is a very poor district. He gathered together nine young men, all with a little education, and offered them three years' hard disciplined work, a systematic training and the possibility to build up a bank balance so that they could settle down to co-operative farming. Two men gave up good urban professional possibilities in order to work in rural development so important to Nigeria. They were thrilled. Now two years later they are growing yams and other crops, and have built large and well-planned yam storage areas rather like the greenhouses at Kew Gardens without the glass. There is also a small irrigation scheme. In a year's time these enthusiastic young men, one or two of them now married, will decide whether they will continue in the co-operative nature of the farming or divide the settlement into nine smallholdings. At present they deduct the cost of living from the proceeds of marketing and the remainder is divided among them and banked with the expectation that they will be able to consolidate their farms and so be completely self-supporting.

The four settlements cover a large area of land separated from each other. The second one I saw, the original project, where there were twelve young men was a very satisfying experience. I was told they were to make decisions about their future the following week. Here there were five hundred hens in a simple but competent set of buildings.

At the moment all the participants in their projects are living in very primitive quarters because they are putting all their energy into the settlements. They look forward to better housing.

Various community development courses are held in the villages. Mr. Hutchison said:

'The Massey-Ferguson 35X has proved very useful in the most rugged conditions and has carried out all the work in bringing new land under mechanised cultivation for the first time. The equipment can be carried conveniently on the trailer to the village farm projects. A tractor driver had to be trained for the work and is now doing an efficient job.'

It was an edifying day. We were delighted to know Christian Aid had made most of this possible and even more so now when further developments had been planned. I expect it disintegrated when the tragic civil war rent Nigeria to pieces.

AN EXPERIENCE BROADENED

My job has taken me several times to the Middle East where the needs of the Arab refugees are great and their situation intolerable. In 1958 I crossed over into Israel as a guest of the Government, into that new Western country vibrant with modern life, set within an ancient world. It is impossible to describe how mixed my feelings were and how difficult it was for my limited understanding to compass the tragedy of this unhappy part of the world.

My heart and mind were full of the desperate need of the million Arab refugees whose camps I had visited many times. How could one fail to understand the Arabs' desire to return to their own homes? But entering Israel brought back all one's memories of Jewish refugees down the centuries—the massacre by the Nazis of five million innocent victims, the little pin-pricks of racial prejudice seen everywhere. No wonder these people feel the desperate need of a homeland and the determination to keep it at all costs.

My concern was to be able to muster enough imagination to see the problems in the right perspective. I felt miserable. I couldn't get the Arabs out of my mind.

Then one afternoon, I was taken to visit an elderly couple who had lost both their sons in one day in the war in 1949. The woman spoke a little English with a strong Russian accent but was anxious for me to read a book she had written in very poor English about her sons. It was called *The Brothers*. A quite remarkable thing happened; at once we met as persons—we sat for hours trying to make our understanding of each other real in spite of the language barrier. I came to know all about those two boys, their hopes, their fears and their family life. We spoke of the political situation on quite a different level because somehow this family of four, two of them dead, had become symbolic of the tragedy of man, not only in the Middle East but everywhere. Through our understanding of each other I began to understand what my attitude should be to the complicated and wider problem.

Perhaps understanding is the hardest of God's gifts to receive. It seems so remote from the tangible world. So often we understand with our minds but are unable to experience that understanding in our personal relationships. Why do I act in one way and you in another in the same situation? So often we lack imagination so that our silences, our jealousies, our indifferences and our refined cruelty to each other stand in the way of really meeting one another. How can we, then, preoccupied with our personal problems, be expected to understand what is happening to people in distant places? It all sounds so complicated that we leave it to the politicians and the experts. We just cannot accept that we belong to one another, however far apart. We find it difficult to believe anyway. And yet understanding—imagination—the intangibles of a spiritual life, are there if we can only find them. Talking to the parents of those two boys gave me a flood of understanding that helped my imagination to function. For a fleeting hour we had a relationship that was a deeply spiritual experience for all of us.

NO MIDNIGHT LONG REMAINS

I thought of these journeys as I listened to the sermon Dr. Martin Luther King gave in 1966 to the Church and Society Conference in Geneva. Because of the riots in Chicago we watched the empty pulpit and heard his voice ring out in the Cathedral as it was transmitted to us behind his photograph televised by Eurovision and all over Europe. I thought of it many times when his tragic death was announced and we watched the funeral on television.

His text was:

> Which of you who has a friend will go to him at midnight and say to him, 'Friend, lend me three loaves; for a friend of mine has arrived on a journey, and I have nothing to set before him'?
>
> Luke 11 : 5–6 RSV

It is midnight within the social order. On the international horizon nations are engaged in a colossal and bitter contest for supremacy. Two world wars have been fought within a generation, and the clouds of another war are dangerously low. Man now has an atomic and nuclear weapon that could within seconds completely destroy the major cities of the world. Yet the arms race continues and nuclear tests still explode in the atmosphere, with the grim prospect that the very air we breathe will be poisoned by radioactive fallout. Will these circumstances and weapons bring the annihilation of the human race?

This midnight in man's external collective life is paralleled by midnight in his interior individual life. It is midnight within the psychological order. Everywhere paralysing fears harrow people by day and haunt them by night. Deep clouds of anxiety and depression are suspended in our mental skies. More people are emotionally disturbed today than at any other time of human history.

It is also midnight within the moral order. At midnight colours lose their distinctiveness and become a sullen shade of grey. Moral principles have lost their distinctiveness. For modern man, absolute right and absolute wrong is a matter of what the majority is doing. Right and wrong are relative to likes and dislikes and the customs of a particular community. We have unconsciously applied Einstein's theory of relativity, which properly described the physical universe, to the moral and ethical realm.

Midnight is the hour when men desperately seek to obey the eleventh commandment, 'Thou shalt not get caught.' According to the ethic of midnight, the cardinal sin is to be caught and the cardinal virtue is to get by. It is all right to lie, but one must lie with real finesse. It is all right to steal, if one is so dignified that, if caught, the charge becomes embezzlement, not robbery. It is permissible even to hate, if one so dresses his hating in the garments of love that hating appears to be loving. The Darwinian concept of the survival of the fittest has been substituted by a philosophy of the survival of the slickest. This mentality has brought a tragic breakdown of moral standards, and the midnight of moral degeneration deepens.

As in the parable, so in our world today, the deep darkness of midnight is interrupted by the sound of a knock. In the door of the Church millions of people knock.

They continue to feel that the Church provides an answer to the deep confusion that encompasses their lives. It is still the one familiar landmark where the weary traveller by midnight comes. It is the one house which stands where it has always stood, the house to which the man travelling at midnight either comes or refuses to come. Some decide not to come. But the many who come and knock are desperately seeking a little bread to tide them over.

When the man in the parable knocked on his friend's door and asked for three loaves of bread, he received the impatient retort, 'Do not bother me; the door is now shut, and my children are with me in bed; I cannot get up and give you anything.' How often have men experienced a similar disappointment when at midnight they knock on the door of the church.

Midnight is a confusing hour when it is difficult to be faithful. The most inspiring word that the Church may speak is that no midnight long remains.

6

HISTORICAL SIGNPOSTS AND PERSONAL COMMENT

JUST BY CHANCE!

How did you manage to get the job? This was a question asked of me, in different words, on many occasions, primarily by women because I was a woman. But I recall this particular phraseology exactly. It was directed at me some years ago in the porch of a church at the end of a meeting which I had addressed on the occasion of the Women's World Day of Prayer. The scarcely veiled half-sneering, half-envious tone of self-righteousness could only be enunciated by one woman to another. I replied, 'Just by chance' She answered 'You were lucky.' She was right. It was by chance and I was lucky.

It happened because there was a crisis when Inter-Church Aid, as it was then, was only eighteen months old. The Board found themselves with no secretary because of illness, owing the bank money and faced with almost certain demise after a brave 'take-over' from the wound-up Christian Reconstruction in Europe. I was just finishing my allotted time with the Youth Department of the British Council of Churches, was leaving and therefore the only person available in sight. The staff was reduced to three persons and they had been warned they might become redundant. I said I would do it for six months. I am often told with tolerant affection by close friends that I am a natural impressario. If it is true using the word within a wider context, then that was what they needed. While only too aware of my limitations in those years, I nevertheless found it satisfying in every sense of the word.

SIDELINES

There has not been room to mention in detail some of the sidelines of Christian Aid. They include the ecumenical student programme, which was started in 1945 and still continues most successfully; it has been extra busy with 'Biafran' students during the Nigerian civil war. Then there was Voluntary Service Overseas, started by Alec Dickson, and for the first three years of its life Christian Aid did the accounts and the administration. When it launched itself independently into the large organisation it is now, Christian Aid decided to do their Youth Volunteer programme through V.S.O. rather than start a new operation. Today a fifth of V.S.O. volunteers are sponsored by Christian Aid. When I retired I was invited to remain on the Council, and gladly accepted. I have always regarded V.S.O. as one of the most satisfying of my interests.

It became quite clear five years ago that Christian Aid must be involved with the immigrant community in this country. An advisory committee was set up in collaboration with the Social Responsibility Department of the British Council of Churches. Money was found to help local community projects and since then it has developed into something larger and more effective.

CO-OPERATION

Christian Aid has had close relations with the United Nations High Commissioner for Refugees and the Food and Agricultural Organisation. Through the good office of the World Council of Churches there has been much coming and going between staff and Christian Aid and its related agencies in other parts of the world. I held several offices on committees in Geneva until the Uppsala Assembly in 1968. We have always co-operated with Save the Children Fund, War on Want, the Red Cross, Oxfam and others. The most notable field of co-operation is in relation to education for economic development, primarily co-ordinated by the Voluntary Committee on Overseas Aid and Development which was set up by the Ministry of Overseas Development. Our closest co-operation is with Oxfam. Leslie Kirkby, the Director, and I were firm friends and colleagues. We had the same problems and met regularly to support each other.

MORE RECENT HAPPENINGS

The civil war in Nigeria started in 1967 therefore I was personally very much involved with aid and relief until 1968. It was a terrible business and we had intimate friends on both sides. Since I retired there has been a most wonderful response by the Churches and this continues now the cease-fire has taken place. Both during the war and since, the World Council of Churches and therefore Christian Aid has worked through the Nigerian Council of Churches. Thousands of pounds have been contributed by the British Churches through Christian Aid and considerable quantities of food and equipment as well as personnel have been made available. To quote Alan Brash in a letter sent to all local Christian Aid organisers on the 23rd January 1970: 'The Churches will continue so long as there is need and so long as we take the gospel seriously.'

Towards the end of 1969 all the Departments of the British Council of Churches, including Christian Aid, the

Roman Catholic Commission on Justice and Peace and the Conference of British Missionary Societies, joined together to organise a 'Sign-in'. The intention was entirely educational, designed to challenge the people of the Churches to decide whether or not they really wished to endorse the Government's decision in principle, that Great Britain give one per cent of the Gross National Product to overseas aid as the Pearson Commission recommended. The publicity was tremendous and sometimes critical as well as mistaken. At the time of writing with fifty per cent of returned signatures there were more than half a million Church members signed.'

Action for World Development is a longer term exercise and a combined operation of eight agencies including Christian Aid, War on Want and Oxfam. In broad terms it is an effort to encourage the ordinary citizens to be involved politically for overseas aid. This endorses the Christian Aid Manifesto agreed by the British Council of Churches that development was a major concern of the Churches and everyone should be urged in their own sphere to press for political action. Already there are over two hundred groups in various parts of the country working to this end. There are, as might have been expected, outspoken criticisms from some local Churches. To quote Alan Brash: 'In answer to our critics, the cost of this activity to Christian Aid is only one-sixth of one per cent of income from non-charitable sources. In spite of the minority that felt Christian Aid was being too political, the majority felt it was being increasingly relevant. On the 31st January 1970, the income was a quarter of a million pounds above the figures at the same date the previous year.' In 1969 the Methodist Church, in consultation with Christian Aid, raised over four hundred thousand pounds for development projects by many members forgoing one day's pay. The Congregational Church and the Presbyterian Church of England are agreed that their members give one per cent of their income for the same object in 1970. Other Churches are considering similar action. All this is over and above what they normally do through Christian Aid Week.

FAITH AND ACTION

These words were written by the United Nations High Commissioner for Refugees in 1954:

It seems to me to be one of the greatest achievements of the Christian Churches in recent times that they have started increasingly to translate their faith and their hope into terms of practical programmes and projects in fields in which they bear responsibility—I do not think that I have any right to compare, but I would be surprised if there were any field in which Christians have achieved so much as they have in the field of the refugee problem.

In 1949 the Central Committee of the World Council of Churches held its first meeting after the First Assembly held in Amsterdam in 1948, at Chichester, under the chairmanship of Dr. George Bell. At the end of the discussion on the function of the Division of Inter-Church Aid and Service to Refugees the final minute included the sentence often quoted: 'Finally the Central Committee decided to remind the member Churches that Inter-Church Aid and Service to Refugees is a permanent obligation of a World Council of Churches which seeks to be true to its name.'

Christian Aid in the British Isles has tried from the beginning to keep that obligation in the forefront of all its activities. Undoubtedly thousands of men and women in the local Churches work for Christian Aid because they see this obligation as relevant when they seek as Christians to tackle world poverty.

The Church today is constantly under attack both from within and without and membership is falling, but the Church cannot dodge its responsibility to face the challenge to care for the 'widows and orphans' in modern terms. Undoubtedly the development of the ecumenical movement has made it more possible. During the last twenty-five years a significant contribution to the alleviation of suffering peoples has been made by Churches all over the world working together through the World Council of Churches. There is now a positive change in relationships between the Roman Catholic Church and the other Churches. Recently the first joint appointment of a staff member was made by the Vatican and the World Council of Churches to be located at the World Council's headquarters in Geneva.

In the early days Inter-Church Aid and Refugee Service had difficulties with its title. Christians as well as non-Christians thought the projects for which we appealed for money were confined to one church helping another. They did not understand that the Churches were helping others in poverty-stricken countries to play a major part in relieving the distress of their nation. As Christian Aid Week became well known, there was even more confusion and so we changed our title to Christian Aid. There was at that time no doubt whatever that we would have attracted more money and support for our educational programmes if we had not had 'Christian' in our title. This is less true today but perhaps our income would by now have been over three million pounds had we yielded to pressure. But it is a fact that the United Nations and governments recognise the tremendous scope of the World Council of Churches Service Agency as being an important and major international aid organisation. This is more significant now that we are working with Roman Catholics. They are seeking to move into more co-ordinated methods of working and they frankly admit that we can help them as they try to work with the World Council, which in respect to co-ordination has progressed much further. Together they play a significant role in demonstrating the value of the influence of the voluntary organisations in the field of aid and development.

I have had more letters from Church members and Christian students than from those outside the Church, suggesting we drop the word 'Christian' in order to avoid the disadvantage of projecting an institution which the critics say is irrelevant in a hungry world. I contend that it is right that the Church should acknowledge its calling as it seeks to serve. I see this as an integral part of the mission of the Church. I find it sad that there are still some Church and missionary society adherents, mostly professing their belief in ecumenical action and mission and unity, proclaiming that Christian Aid is only a relief agency and therefore a separate entity from the Churches' mission in the world. I have rarely met this attitude when travelling in Asia, Africa and Latin America, engaged in discussing plans for projects with the indigenous leaders of the Churches. What is relief anyway? I see Christian Aid as picking up the man on the road to Jericho, asking the innkeeper to feed him and paying him to do so, and then going to Jerusalem and making conditions both politically and socially possible, for that man and others like him, to help themselves and so discourage thieves and robbers by providing a better standard of living.

Thoughtful Christians accept the fact that while we

live within a Christian culture the majority of the population are not Christian and have no sense of guilt about their agnosticism or total rejection, but there are many who find satisfaction and fulfilment on the periphery of the Church. They see Christian Aid and service programmes in general and its expression of the life of Jesus Christ as something they understand. They will take a lot of persuading that that is not enough, but they believe in 'Christian compassion' and expect the Church to be practical; thus they are torn between the world they know and the desire for something larger.

This attitude is developing in the Churches overseas where we have taken the gospel, enclosed within our Western culture and traditions, which would often seem to be on the surface an essential element of organised Christianity. Dramatic changes are taking place, not least because most of these countries are basically rooted in other religions and they, as well as the countries in the West, are becoming pluralistic societies. It is difficult to persuade even Church people who are serious about world poverty, that in some ways we waste more money than we give or raise for overseas aid or for those in need at home, on maintaining innumerable half-empty churches. We also waste our under-paid manpower and at the same time indulge in long-drawn-out discussions on unity. Ordinary people, both within and without the Church, understand that Jesus Christ spoke a common language in his day which was relevant to people beset with fear and hopelessness, and which had nothing to do with being enslaved to particular traditions but to man's need. When, more often than is supposed, the Church is true to itself and the care for those in need is seen to be a priority of the Church, it is acknowledged by those outside to be relevant and its witness in the world more understood.

A poem by Salvatore Quasimodo[1] gets to the heart of the matter:

'Man of My Time'

You are still the man of the stone and sling,
man of my time. You were in the cockpit
with malignant wings, dials of death
—I have seen you—in the chariot of fire, at
the gallows,
at the wheels of torture. I have seen you: it
was you,
your exact science turned to extermination,
without love, without Christ. You have killed again,
as always, as your fathers killed, as they killed
the animals that saw them for the first time.
And the blood smells the same as when
a brother told his brother: 'Let us go
to the fields.' And that echo, chill, insistent,
has reached you, down to your day.
Sons, forget the clouds of blood
risen from the earth, forget your fathers:
their tombs sink down in ashes:
the black birds, the wind, cover their heart.

Frequently in national and local ecumenical circles the debates on mission and service, on mission and unity, on racialism, on peace and war, on development, on the Church in the world today, are couched either in language that is too academic or in words so radical that many ordinary people in the pews find both incomprehensible. In spite of this I believe the World Council of Churches and the impatience of the young people of the Church and some theologians, are beginning to influence

[1] *The Listener* 6th July, 1967.

Christians all over the world. Christian Aid and its equivalent in other countries has had a reconciling influence in Churches, especially those who are experimenting in practical action calling for new structures and change.

The young people marching, protesting and singing their songs or new types of hymns, may not seem to politicians and scholars to contribute to statesmen-like development, but nevertheless we are all influenced by them and undoubtedly their revolution will profoundly affect the future pattern of Church and society in the not too distant future. Sidney Carter, the folk singer, wrote a song for Christian Aid, the refrain being 'When I needed a neighbour, were you there, were you there? And the creed and the colour and the name won't matter, were you there?' This has been sung by thousands of young people all over Britain, and while often we are still not there if the creed and the colour are not to our liking the increasing concern in the Churches for a hungry world is encouraging and hopeful.

Dietrich Bonhoeffer said: 'To allow the hungry man to remain hungry would be blaspheming against God and one's faith.' While I think he meant physical hunger, it surely also means man's hunger for understanding and love, hunger for freedom of spirit and thought, hunger for political freedom, hunger for a spiritual outlet within his way of life and his limitations. If this is true, then Christian Aid is not just another charity but should be a reconciling factor in the Church and the world, between nationality, classes and between Christian and non-Christian. Feeding hungry men is the common concern of all men, whatever their language or their belief, and in my opinion this is an essential pioneering process towards mission and unity.

NEED NOT CREED

Christian Aid is a modern organisation and as such is officially only twenty-one years old. But its creation was a stage in the development of an ecumenical and international process started forty-eight years ago. In general its objects were to care for refugees, the hungry millions in Asia, Africa and Latin America, the homeless, the unwanted and the victims of discrimination whatever their creed or none everywhere.

More recently and more precisely Christian Aid has declared its determination to be at the heart of community and economic development in every continent but especially in the so-called 'third world'. It seems to me therefore that it is essential to indicate briefly the outstanding dates in the history of the Churches' response to the world-wide call for aid, by those in need in a century of rapid social change and violent upheaval.

In 1922 Adolf Keller, a Swiss Protestant, became the Director of the European Bureau for Inter-Church Aid. It was started by the Swiss Protestant Church and the Federal Council of the Churches of Christ in America. There were still large numbers of stateless persons, remnants of the victims of the First World War, needing special resettlement possibilities and security of nationality. At the same time Church World Service was founded in the United States of America to help the starving millions in China after severe droughts and widespread failure of crops.

In 1937 China was again the object of help because of the Japanese invasion.

From 1933 to 1939 the Bureau went to work urgently and internationally for the Jews fleeing from Hitler and Nazi persecution. During this period in the British Isles, the Bishop of Chichester, Dr. George Bell, led Christians and their friends in an intensive effort to help Jews to get out of Germany and into this country. He not only played a prominent part in finding them jobs and homes, he also agitated politically to ensure that they had a fair deal when the war started and panic measures resulted in discrimination and distress among the refugees.

In 1942 the British Council of Churches was established.

During the early years of the war the World Council of Churches, which was in 'Process of Formation', had a small office in Geneva and was already organising international work for prisoners of war. It was also making plans for a united effort by the Churches to help the millions of refugees and displaced persons, who it was assumed would be found in concentrated areas of Europe after the cessation of hostilities.

In 1945 Inter-Church Aid, in collaboration with National Church Agencies such as Church World Service in the United States and Christian Reconstruction Committees in Switzerland, Great Britain, Canada, Australia and many other countries, carried out enormous works of relief and rehabilitation. They also helped the Churches in Germany, Austria and Italy and the countries occupied during the war to renew their life.

From 1945 to 1949 Christian Reconstruction in the British Isles decided to make a Million Pound Fund Appeal. At that time rationing was still prevalent in this country, including bread and potatoes. This object was completed by 1949. The Church of England raised £250,000, the same amount provided by the other denominations, and nearly a million pounds by the 'co-operating societies', which included the Y.M.C.A., the Y.W.C.A., the British and Foreign Bible Society, the Student Christian Movement and several other ecumenical organisations.

In 1945 the World Council of Churches set up an Ecumenical Refugee Commission and opened a London office.

In 1948 the First Assembly of the World Council of Churches was held in Amsterdam. After the reports of Inter-Church Aid and the Refugee Commission were presented to the Assembly, it was unanimously agreed that there could not be a World Council without a service arm, to provide for the hungry and the refugees. In 1954 the Second Assembly was held in Evanston, Illinois.

In 1948 the first meeting of the World Council's Central Committee met in Chichester under the Chairmanship of Dr. George Bell and a Division was created to be called Inter-Church Aid and Service to Refugees. It was resolved that this should be a permanent obligation. At the Third Assembly in New Delhi in 1960 it changed its name to the Division of Inter-Church Aid Refugee and World Service.

In 1949 the British Council of Churches set up a Department of Inter-Church Aid and Refugee Service.

In 1957 the first Christian Aid Week took place in two hundred towns and villages and £26,000 was the result. This was during the time of the Hungarian revolution when all the rooms in the headquarters of the British Council of Churches were crowded with Hungarian refugees. They were sitting on the stairs and lying about in the corridor and every room in the building was full. But in spite of the difficulties the rather indifferent organisation of the Christian Aid Week went ahead.

In 1964 the Department of Inter-Church Aid and Refugee Service became 'Christian Aid'. Its income had been £20,000 in *1952* and in *1969* it was two and a half million pounds, and educational material was by then a major part of the operation.

In 1968 the Fourth Assembly of the World Council of Churches took place in Uppsala, Sweden, when the member churches agreed, together with the Roman Catholic Church, to make development a major concern.

Throughout, the Roman Catholic Church had similar service activities all over the world. In the immediate post-war years it was only in the refugee camps in Europe and the resettlement offices in most continents that they worked together. Since 1965 there have been regular consultations in Rome and Geneva on development projects and the necessity for education about economic development, joint appeals and co-operative efforts planned for the future. For some years many Roman Catholics in the British Isles have supported Christian Aid Week and now are on most of the two thousand local planning committees as well as participating in the wider activities of a large number of local Councils of Churches.

Three Hundred Years of Missionary Outreach

The Missionary Societies of most of the Western Churches were the real pioneers of the service agencies. As well as taking the gospel to non-Western lands they were the forerunners of medical, educational, agricultural and social work in many parts of the world where previously such services were unknown. At first in some 'missionary' areas and within Missionary Societies there was suspicion of the large sophisticated service organisations moving into Asia, Africa and Latin America with increased aid, often more related to governments than Churches. These suspicions are now almost entirely eradicated and there is an effective working partnership in development programmes and refugee relief. Without the overseas experience of the missionaries it would have

186

been difficult for the Christian Service Agencies to have made anything like the large contribution to world need which they have been privileged to do.

Ecumenical Service Agencies

The one World Council of Churches Division that is accepted by most people, Christian and non-Christian alike, is the Division of Inter-Church Aid, Refugee and World Service. This makes sense. It is thoroughly scriptural in its concept and action. There have been radical changes in the attitude of many Churches in the last twenty years not only in the more ready acceptance of aid with love, and with no strings attached, but also in ecumenical outlook.

I remember in 1954 at the height of the Mau Mau revolution visiting some remote villages in the reserves. I had attended several small Christian services, each different in their type of worship and theological assumptions but united in their tribal community and religious language. My escort, a highly intelligent and liberal priest, was driving at breakneck speed in the falling dusk, through heavily wooded country, so that we might reach the 'safety' area before we were enclosed in black darkness. I asked him why it was not explained to the groups that we had visited that there was not one Church, but many. 'What,' I asked, 'would be the effect on some of the Kikuyu in the villages when eventually they went to Nairobi or London, and saw for themselves that the one Western Church of Jesus Christ was many Churches terribly separate?' He replied, 'Oh, it would never do, it is much too complicated.' I marvelled silently, that in a country torn apart by bloody revolution, the very reconciling unity that is the essence of the teaching of Jesus, seemed to a devout and sincere Christian to be too complicated to proclaim.

This book is primarily about the British part in a world-wide ecumenical service to millions of people in desperate need. The scope and significance of this remarkable development since 1945 has been possible only because it was international. Therefore I must mention briefly, and inevitably inadequately, the sister agencies with whom Christian Aid has co-operated from the beginning.

The largest ecumenical agency in Europe is German Hilfswerk, a well-organised and comprehensive organisation collecting considerable funds from the Churches and sending many highly competent experts to the developing countries. Hilfswerk was founded in 1945 by Dr. Eugene Gerstemeir at a time when we were sending considerable quantities of food, other necessities and personnel to Germany. The largest Protestant Christian Service Agency in the World is Church World Service U.S.A., now approaching its golden jubilee. After the Second World War they received nearly a million European refugees and are still doing the same today from other parts of the world. The millions of dollars every year collected by the American Churches, tremendous quantities of food, clothing and medicaments, as well as a considerable number of men and women serving abroad is most impressive.

But these are only two examples of a great number in every continent. It is difficult to select a few for mention and to exclude so many more known to me intimately, but they include the considerable United Christian relief organisation in India, Korea, Brazil, the Middle East, Kenya and smaller service agencies in almost every African and Asian country. They are to be found in almost every country in Europe and one must highlight Swiss Hilfswerk and the Scandinavian Inter-Church Aid organisations. Naturally some are more active than others but basically they are all the same. Practically all are working closely with Roman Catholic organisations and within their own governmental community development programmes, as well as being related to the United Nations. They provide a remarkable chain of international bodies working for those in need, agitating together for peace and justice, and bringing pressure to bear for increased economic development in the third world. All this is planned and co-ordinated through the World Council of Churches. There is at all times close collaboration with Lutheran World Service.

A PERSONAL COMMENT

It was a great joy to me when Alan Brash accepted the offer to succeed me in 1968 as Director of Christian Aid. He was an old friend and colleague and I am sad that he has been 'translated' to the World Council of Churches to be Director of the Division of Inter-Church Aid Refugee and World Service after two years in office. He has made a significant contribution to the ecumenical movement in these islands as well as to Christian Aid. I quote a letter from him just as he was leaving London. 'I want to say to you for you to interpret as you will that everything which is of value which has happened since you left is substantially the fruit of the foundations which you laid and the work which you undertook. It is your achievement that you built Christian Aid from £20,000 to £1,500,000; it is also the effect of the solidity of your work that in the first year after your departure the figure was increased to £2,500,000. Whatever you do about publishing this statement, the fact remains that there has been no basic change in policy and no radical reorientation in direction, but that we have pressed on, using the opportunities of the moment as they were increased following Vatican II and Uppsala, challenging the Churches to direct denominational action through ecumenical channels, with the result that we have really become an agency of major dimensions as a result of the direction and impetus which was provided during the formative years when you were Director.'

I quote this not out of any feeling of pride but of gratitude for the continuing progress of Christian Aid and for the opportunity that was mine when working with Christian Aid, and a sense of relief that foundations laid in years of struggle have grown so satisfactorily. The Rev. Alan Booth has been appointed as the new Director of Christian Aid. He is a well known and experienced ecumenical figure and his international experience will add new dimensions to Christian Aid. I continue to give talks on economic development and enjoy the friendship of Christian Aid colleagues, to whom I owe so much.

In a curious way my different experiences have come full circle because for six months I have been working temporarily with the Family Welfare Association as Acting Director. Thus, I am back on the home front where there is a tremendous need. I have promised to stay for at least another year to help reorganise the structure and administration of a century-old organisation needing a 'new look'. I find myself once again calling on my past experience and using the familiar technique of starting with fundamentals and building up for the future.

I could have wished I had had the opportunity to take a more vigorous part in politics, but I am more interested in battling with political issues, rather than professional party strategy, which has its limitations. Professionalism means being trained and paid to perform a function but, fundamentally, it is an attitude of mind which is the real

basis of professionalism. This I have endeavoured to
provide in everything I have undertaken.

> *The Spirit of the Lord* GOD *is upon me,*
> *because the* LORD *has anointed me*
> *to bring good tidings to the afflicted;*
> *he has sent me to bind up the brokenhearted,*
> *to proclaim liberty to the captives,*
> *and the opening of the prison to those*
> *who are bound;*
> *to proclaim the year of the* LORD'S *favour,*
> *and the day of vengeance of our God;*
> *to comfort all who mourn;*
> *to grant to those who mourn in Zion—*
> *to give them a garland instead of ashes,*
> *the oil of gladness instead of mourning*
> *the mantle of praise instead of a faint spirit;*
> *that they may be called oaks of righteousness,*
> *the planting of the* LORD, *that he may*
> *be glorified.*
> *They shall build up the ancient ruins,*
> *they shall raise up the former devastations;*
> *they shall repair the ruined cities,*
> *the devastations of many generations.*